the macro world of micro cars

kate trant and austin williams

Black Dog Publishing

Contents

Foreword   **5**

by Stephen Bayley

Introduction   **6**

Chapter One   **9**
The Political Framework

don't mention the war   12

micro-economics and mini-marts   18

the bubble bursts   25

microclimates   32

endnotes   38

Chapter Two   **39**
The Contemporary Culture Of Microcars

owners and clubs   43

record breakers   45

collectors and collecting   48

The People   **54**

endnotes   92

Chapter Three   **93**
Good Things Come In Small Packages

necessity is the mother of invention   102

entrepreneurs and designers   106

marketing and press   107

AC Petite   112

Berkeley   113

BMW Isetta   115

Bond Bug   118

Bond Minicar Mark A-G   119

Crosley   121

Fiat Topolino 500A   122

Fiat 600   123

Fiat Nuova 500   125

Fiat Stationwagon   127

Frisky   128

Glas Goggomobil T250-TS400   130

Heinkel and Trojan 200   132

Lloyd Alexander   133

Messerschmitt KR200 and TG500   135

Nobel 200   137

L'Oeuf   139

Opperman Unicar and Opperman Stirling   140

Peel P50   141

Piaggio Ape   142

Reliant Regal Mark I-VI   143

Rovin D2   145

Scootacar (Mark 1) and DeLuxe (Mark 11)   146

Sinclair C5   148

Smart   151

Subaru 360   152

Vespa 400   154

Zündapp Janus   157

endnotes   158

Chapter Four   **159**
Thinking Small

endnotes   169

bibliography   174

index   175

The Macro World of Microcars

Foreword

Small cars are more interesting than large cars. The dimensions may not be so great, but the creative challenges are bigger. First, there is the question of proportions: a large car gives a stylist more scope, more lines to play with, more space to occupy, more money to spend, more stuff to consume. The aesthetics of small cars are hobbled by pinched relationships of material to space. This is just one reason why there has never been a truly beautiful small car and designers have to take refuge in a different artistic destination. This is why there have been lots of extremely cute small cars. And in a harsh world, cute is good. Show me the man who says a Ford Crown Victoria is cute and I will show you a man with a bad case of cognitive dissonance.

Second, there is the packaging. The dimensional limitations force ingenuity: if you have very little to play with, you do not squander it. Third, the engineering. To achieve acceptable results with small means calls for disciplined thought and ingenious solutions. Stringent criteria like these do not intimidate designers, they inspire them. As Sir Joshua Reynolds knew, as he laid down the law about painting to his fellow Royal Academicians, "rules are not an impediment to genius, but an inspiration to it". And the rule of size is the most demanding.

So there are more small cars illustrating the history of design than there are stretch limos. One of the most beautiful images I know is a cross-section of Dante Giacosa's original Fiat Cinquecento of 1936, a masterful arrangement of metal and air in space that is a diagram of Le Corbusier's belief that "good design is intelligence made visible". From the same moment, Pierre Boulanger's and Flaminio Bertoni's Citroen 2CV showed that minimal means can—when working with a Bauhaus credo and a strict brief—achieve a maximal result. The Deux Chevaux was simple and small, but proved these are not definitions of privation rather pointers to a radical definition of comfort. At the same time, Porsche's Volkswagen proved that a small car could be engineered to standards hitherto the selfishly guarded province of the large car. And the most influential car of all time? This was the one that gave the world a new word: "mini". Alec Issigonis' creation had more innovation than the entire history of the automobile before 1959.

But these are just the most successful small cars. Some of the failures have as much constructive charm and exercise our emotions because they express forlorn and frustrated ambitions. The Kleinschnittger F125 of 1950 would be an example. And so would the 1955 Suzuki Suzulight. Even the atrocious Bond Bug of 1970 deserves its place in the history of ambition as much as it deserves to be remembered by the scorch marks its burnt-out plastic shells left on the dual carriage-ways of Britain.

The best small cars are authentic design classics, although they are shunned by the classic car set, a tribe that does not, on the whole, worship at the altar of *Existenzminimum*. I know this because I had an authentic classic car of my own, one of the last Cinquecentos. It was unreliable. It was slow, frustrating, dangerous and uncomfortable. But it made me smile. Every day. And you cannot say that about a Ferrari.

Stephen Bayley

Introduction

The era of the microcar was a relatively fleeting moment in the history of the motorcar, now more than a century old. A regular and acceptable feature on the roads in the 1950s, their popularity had well and truly waned by the end of the Swinging 60s. But recently there has been a confident resurgence in small cars, and what have become known as 'city cars'. So, is there a common thread linking these typologies? What was it that the microcar represented in its heydays, and how does it compare with its status today? This is the first time that a critical history of the microcar up to the present day has been undertaken.

Various attempts have been made to explain the microcar phenomenon. Chris Rees, in *Microcar Mania: The definitive history of the small car*, states that microcars came into existence "offering motoring for the masses in the case of cyclecars in 1920-1925; overcoming raw material shortages in the case of the post war bubble cars; and alleviating the pressures of chokingly congested traffic and dwindling fuel reserves of modern times".

This sounds like a reasonable description of three key periods of the twentieth century: pre war, immediate post war and 'modern' (i.e. the latter half of the twentieth century), but it doesn't really get to the heart of the matter. Effectively, most critiques simply look at the microcar from the perspective of consumption, especially in relation to shortages: shortages of affordable alternatives in the inter war years, of manufacturing capability in the post war period and shortages of resources and roadbuildng in the present period. But there is more to it than tales of scarcity and deficiency.

What microcars *reflect* (in terms of material rationing, social austerity, financial constraints, etc.) is one thing, but the purpose of this book is to explain what they represent. What mood, what aspiration—what 'moment'—did the growth and demise of microcars capture in the past and what does the new generation of microcars say about the period in which we now live? Rather than exploring what history says about microcars, we want to explore what the history of microcars say about ourselves: our past, present and, to a large extent, our future.

As in all contributions to public discourse, we stand above the parapet to be shot at. However, in an attempt to get some retaliation in early, we note that brevity has necessitated the use of some bald assertions throughout the course of the book. It has also been difficult to assess the true significance of the microcar—in terms of its penetration into the 'normal' car market—through tracing registration numbers. In the UK, it was only in 1974 that the Driver and Vehicle Licensing Authority (DVLA) began registering and licensing all new vehicles. They note that by 1983, "the Department was facing grave problems associated with the forgery of old style log books and fraudulent claims to attractive registration marks. The solution lay in calling a halt to the continuing registration of old vehicles under their original mark." A lot of the traceability of purchase records has disappeared in this process. Manufacturers too have lost or misplaced records or their manufacturing bases have closed down. Therefore we acknowledge that after researching public records we have also had to rely, to some extent, on individual speculation and hearsay evidence as to actual numbers, availability and popularity of the microcar.

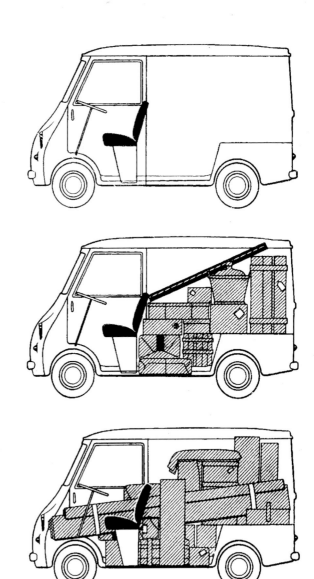

We also know that there are enthusiasts out there who may have gripes about our choice of microcars and also the timescale of our enquiry. Tony Marshall points out that a microcar "cannot be defined with complete certainty" after all, when is a mini a micro?[1] Why wasn't the 1913 Peugeot Bebe included as the earliest microcar? At 855cc and weighing only 405kg, surely it qualifies? We have taken the view that at 2.6 metres long, it fell way outside the usual criteria for the microcar, just as the Austin Seven "Chummy" of the inter war years. Both small-engined small cars perhaps, but not microcars in our book. Similarly, the Mini Cooper, with an engine size of 1.6 litres can't really be considered a microcar in the generally accepted use of the term. Autocar called it "a noteworthy breakthrough in small car design". But even though it's not really that small, it has to be admitted that the Mini does play a key role in the story of the modern microcar which is why we have addressed its particular tale without pandering to the notion that this is what historic microcars are about.

The following chapters will, each in its own style, examine the prevalent political and social mood across the decades—empathetically touching on the nostalgia, humour (and folly) of microcar manufacture in the latter part of the last century and its revival at the beginning of the new. In Chapter One Austin Williams looks at the bigger socio-economic and political picture, starting with the immediate post war era. Appropriating the history of microcars as an adept analysis of the war economy, the growth of micro-production, and the rise of sustainability and environmentalism, it offers a truly global take on the microcar phenomenon.

The following chapter celebrates the people behind the machines: not the designers and manufacturers but the owners. Kate Trant and photographer David Cowlard have tracked down those who lavish care and attention on their beloved motors and documented empathetic stories of people, machines and desires—honouring the great tradition of the love of motoring and of lovable motoring eccentricity.

In Chapter Three, Kate Trant examines the ways in which the cars were designed, and marketed to their potential buyers. It outlines the work of a number of those involved in microcar design, illustrating the development of 30 individual microcar marques as 'family' stories.

In the concluding chapter, Austin Williams draws together the range of issues and questions thrown up in the course of writing this book. It also looks forward to new small car technology that closely correlates with the positive aspiration that was the hallmark of the 1950s.

"The term 'microcar' is an assumed one with no basis in *officialese*. For this reason it cannot be defined with complete certainty, and the question of just what constitutes a microcar is one that can be discussed at length without ever reaching a clear conclusion.... The most commonly held view is that microcars are vehicles built after the end of the Second World War, usually with economy of construction and of use as the main criteria. Microcars can have either three wheels or four, and power is usually provided by an internal combustion engine, though battery electric propulsion is not unknown. Where petrol is the fuel, the engines are often of the two-stroke type which, with fewer parts, are less expensive to produce. Most manufacturers of microcars tended to use power units that were already in production for other applications, with or without modification. The maximum engine displacement for a microcar is generally agreed to be 700cc. Certain microcars fall under the generic term 'bubble cars'. This is a self-explanatory term dating from the 1950s when these cars—principally the Messerschmitt, Heinkel (later Trojan) and Isetta—were available new, and derives from the rounded design styles and large window areas of the vehicles. Hence, bubble cars all come under the heading of microcars, but the reverse is less often the case."

Tony Marshall, *Microcars*

Chapter One
The Political Framework

the political framework

Dai Williams on his Royal Enfield Twin.

I was rumoured to have been conceived in the back of a Baby Austin just as the 1950s were coming to an end. I guess that my name was a foregone conclusion and I regularly thank god that we didn't have a Cortina or a Minx or a Messerschmitt.

My dad had owned a Royal Enfield 500 Twin but made the natural progression to an AJS 500cc, haring around the B-roads with his quiff blowing in the breeze and my mother holding on pillion for dear life. If Benedek's *The Wild Ones*, 1953, hadn't been banned in Britain until 1968 he might have identified with Marlon Brando on his 1950 Triumph Thunderbird 6T rebelling against anything that was on offer. As it was, the movie never came to the Tonypandy Empire, he conformed to the transport hierarchy, and by 1955 the bike was replaced by the Austin Seven and then a Big Eight. In 1960, he moved up to a Ford Popular—a 'proper car' at last.

As our family *double-de-clutched* along, the sight of a bubble car was always a rare treat, but my dad wouldn't have been seen dead in one. Small family cars like ours were at least credible and were seen as a stepping-stone toward escaping the world of a biker's exposure to the elements. People aspired to travel relatively comfortably and speedily in a small car. Here, drizzle was only a nuisance for visibility whereas previously it was a threat to the Brylcreme.

The end of the 1950s heralded the time when an ordinary working class family could actually start to take holidays and explore further afield in affordable comfort. In 1959, in the sufficiently faraway universe of the British Motor Corporation in Birmingham, Alec Issigonis had just finished his masterwork: the 848cc Morris Mini Minor. This was the beginning of a time when the world seemed to undergo rapid change—and for the better—releasing a post war generation from the chains of its parochial surroundings. In the USA, Frank Sinatra released *High Hopes* and in the UK, the Minister of Transport and Aviation, Ernest Marples, was cutting the ribbon on Britain's first motorway.

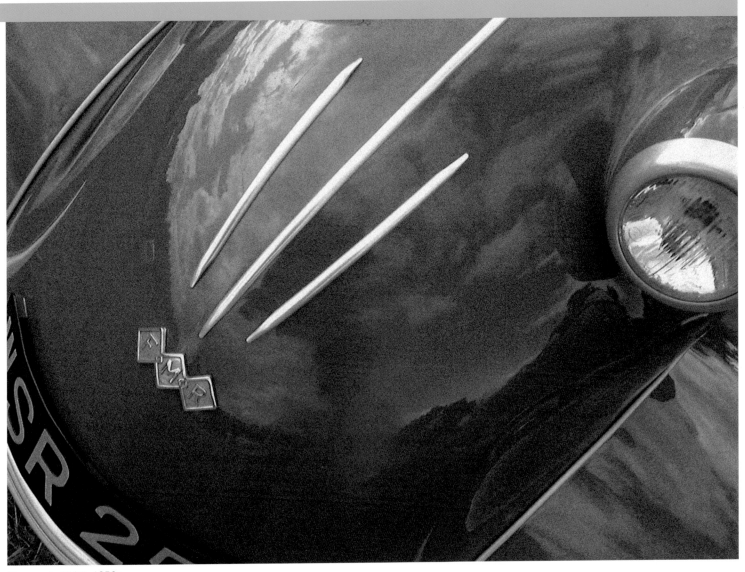

Messerschmitt, late 1950s.

The excitement of an economy being able, allegedly, to meet demand with supply effectively meant that I had been born at the moment of the microcar's ultimate demise. Demand for tiny vehicles dried up when people didn't have to have them. But the aspiration for personal mobility and transport liberation that microcars—in microcosm—provided, was to prove invaluable to the future generations of motor manufacture. Unfortunately, or as some might say, fortunately, microcars were expendable at the time. When the material conditions for their existence were removed, they disappeared voluntarily, gracefully and, apart from a few notable exceptions, with commendable dignity.

Demand for tiny vehicles dried up when people didn't have to have them.

On the European mainland, not much was being built and what there was just wasn't very good.

There is a common misconception that the animosities of war are intractable. For some this is undoubtedly true, but the nationalistic motivations that had pertained for a long time before World War Two were no longer applicable to the new conditions. Esteemed motoring journalist and historian, LJK Setright notes that in 1948 "the idea of buying a German or Japanese car would have been as unthinkable, in the aftermath of the War, as it would have been inadvisable technically".[1] This second point reflects more accurately the real reasons for the official rejection of foreign goods by the Allies in the immediate post war period. After all, the victor can often appear to be magnanimous, it's just that on the European mainland, not much was being built and what there was just wasn't very good.

Britain was rebuilding its export economy and it was the national duty to keep one's belt tightened. There was no real Japanese car industry to speak of, and Germany was in thrall to the United States (Germany had just been allowed to take back the decimated VW plant in Wolfsburg from American control and by the end of the 1940s was allowed to produce only a short run of motorbikes). Any aversion to foreign goods therefore, was premised on pragmatic decisions about deliverability which is distinct from, say, the anti-Japanese car protests by British and American trade unions and manufacturers in the 1980s, based as it was on Western industrial decline and dislike of the competition—all wrapped up with a hint of parochial racism. In the years after the war, there was really nothing new filtering onto the UK market and most ordinary motoring consumers had to choose from pre war models. People with discernment simply wanted something new.

The two most recognisable names in microcar history, which emerged during the 1950s, were the Messerschmitt and the Heinkel, names that are immutably linked (even now) with the German wartime aviation industry.

Paradoxically then, after all that we've been led to believe about national hatred, there was no real hostility towards the German and Japanese business model after Nürnberg. Admittedly, there wasn't much of a German or Japanese business model *at all* until the end of the 1940s, but what there was, operated creatively (employing skilled aeronautical engineers who's industry had been eradicated by Allied dictat) and utilised limited resources efficiently and imaginatively. This goes some way to reconcile the fact that the two most recognisable names in microcar history, which emerged during the 1950s, were the Messerschmitt and the Heinkel, names that are immutably linked (even now) with the German wartime aviation industry. It is interesting, and somewhat instructive, that during this time they could become such accepted names in the world of motoring through the emergence of microcar design.

Heinkel, circa 1956.

Moreover, the Volkswagen Beetle (or 'Bug') designed by Ferdinand Porsche for Adolf Hitler in the mid 1930s, truly became the 'peoples car'—an instantly recognisable curiosity, from Europe to India and South America. It sold only 630 between rolling off the production line in 1940 and the end of the War, by which time its production plant was in ruins. As part of the structured ignominy of defeat, like most of Germany's productive capacity, its facilities were administered by the Allies until 1947. At that point, 20 per cent of its 8,500 output was exported, largely to the US and the rest of Europe.[2] In 1949 the production facility was handed back to German ownership and the first two 'German' cars were exported to America. By the 1950s it was opening up production units all over the world.

Heinkel marketing literature, circa 1956.

Goggomobil, circa 1956.

So when the Messerschmitt and the Heinkel microcars muscled their way in to create and satisfy an entirely new car market, it was the performance, efficiency and cost that people looked to above all else. For people laying out money for a car, technology and technical know-how was appreciated wherever it came from. In the late 1940s, very few dwelt on the past, it was a closed chapter. If it was German and it worked and was, in addition, cost-effective, no questions were asked. In general, microcar purchasers simply enjoyed—as do the fans of the original, and the converts to the upgraded Beetle—that the German marque meant reliable engineering. The distinctive Volkswagen brought reliable performance within reach of many people's pockets. For anyone not in that financial bracket, the reliability (if not the actual physical stability) of a Messerschmitt would be guaranteed. The German national stereotype for rigour was realised in its engineering excellence.[3]

Was there then really a harmonious response to global reconstruction and the German marque? Well, undoubtedly there was still a faint hangover of the War for some, encouraging the Volkswagen production facility to drop the *Kraft durch Freunde* label.[4] But as the Nürnberg war trials came to an end, it was only the more tabloid-esque 'Achtung Tommy!' and 'Take That Fritz!'-style comics in Britain that continued the gung-ho war sentiment.[5] From the late 1940s, when West Germany was created, until the late 1960s, Germany became an accepted and respected player in motor manufacture and industrial reconstruction generally. Indeed, by the 1966 World Cup, Emma Peel was pouring herself voluptuously into a Messerschmitt KR201 in *The Avengers* as a sign of the new *détente*.[6]

Heinkel, circa 1956.

On the other side of the world, the Japanese Ministry of Trade and Industry (MITI) was set up with the intention of replicating Germany's 'people car'. *Kei-jidosha* or *keicars* (small passenger vehicles) were originally built in small numbers and were regulated at 2.8 metres length and 1 metre width to qualify for tax and insurance relaxations. With the country's developing economy, partly prompted by America's 'relentless hostile' attitude towards China, their original low specification motor cars were swiftly superseded by those aspiring to conform with international technical standards.[7] Even the *keicars* grew. However, the Japanese observed and appropriated Western technological advances for their own ends: ingenious technical adaptations but with few presentational niceties. The 'Made in Japan' stamp tended to be a laughing matter in the early 1960s, referring to cheap imitation toys pretending to be something that they weren't. Plastic soldiers in Lucky Bags were the poor boys' die-casts. If 'popular for the people' meant 'inexpensive' then Japan was producing *Volks-everything*. The jokey insults thrown at the products were often borne of Western nervousness at the steady rise of Japanese industry and its ability to produce quickly and profitably. From its origins, Japanese auto firms were considered to be 'fringe competitors' in the US car market of the 1950s. In the 1960s, some still saw their involvement and their potential influence as 'insignificant' but from a standing start they managed to increase market share to 11.74 per cent by the mid-1970s.[8] 30 years later, amidst a period of clinical depression amongst traders about their domestic recessionary climate, business in both Europe and the US began to look to Japan for inspiration. Whether in lean production, JIT delivery or paternalistic management techniques, Japan was reinvented for desperate Western capitalists' consumption. "Europeans, Japanese, and others made their pilgrimage to Detroit from 1920 to 1960, now those who wish to understand the future of industry and economy must visit and study Japan."[9]

"To me it was the excitement of all time to have these beautiful, beautiful cars that I could see, that I could touch, that I could smell...."
Byron Bloch

All the positive things that typified American progressiveness in the 1950s and 1960s–brashness, bigness, conspicuous consumption, social aspiration, etc.–are now seen as no-nos in the post Cold War Order.

The original microcars were small cars for people who were thinking big.

To some, the American model is now seen as the problem primarily because of what it is seen to represent. All the positive things that typified American progressiveness in the 1950s and 1960s–brashness, bigness, conspicuous consumption, social aspiration, etc.–are now seen as no-nos in the post Cold War Order. At the time, even road safety crusader Byron Bloch could say that "I loved the music and I loved the cars of the 1950s, they were so exciting to me. I would sneak in to the car dealerships every fall just to get the first glimpse of the new models....To me it was the excitement of all time to have these beautiful, beautiful cars that I could see, that I could touch, that I could smell...."[10]

Until the 80s 'greed was good' but now the phrase might translate as 'greed is unsustainable'. So it's not really America that's the problem, many liberals say, but it's what America stands for. Unfortunately, what these commentators are rejecting is the very progressive instinct in terms of science, global reach, authority and modernity that exemplified the best in the twentieth century. This book has no remit for American politics, but I hope to try to reclaim an understanding that the US stereotype which is being popularly undermined today is the very thing that encouraged people to move from no-car to microcar to 'proper' car–way back in the middle of the last century. The current tendency to rubbish the gains of modernity–the essence of what many have called the American Dream–is driving the current fad for the new generation of microcars. Microcars today are reflections of how small an impact humanity can have on the planet. This is new. The original microcars were small cars for people who were thinking big; today the equivalent small car is justified less by aspirational mobility questions but by moral restraint. Responsible motoring encourages us to think small, think local, think prudently... think about whether we should be walking instead of taking a car in the first place!

Of course, some might argue that there were plenty of standard family saloons being built by the beginning of the 1950s. Microcars were a marginal player in the grand scheme of things. The Peel Trident, for instance had a production run of no more than 50! Meanwhile, big family cars like the American Ford Zephyrs, France's Citroën DS, Britain's Vauxhall Cresta, Germany's Volkswagen Karmann and even Italy's original Fiat Multipla were being made in some numbers (77,000 Multiplas were produced by 1960). So, in some ways, generalising social trends from the marginal market share of microcars might be seen as slightly disingenuous. But rather than explore a technical story about the progression of an industry, this chapter is looking at what I believe to be the more interesting social trends that underpin it. The fact that General Motors and Ford in America had cancelled their small car plans in 1946 (sic!) says more about their social status and what image they wanted to portray than the straightforward fact that they could only make $100 or $200 profit over the large cars already in production. At the time when big was beautiful, Ford said, "it seems reasonable to ask–if we need a smaller car, do we need a smaller refrigerator or a smaller washing machine?"[11] In those days, the question was rhetorical, the answer, for America, was an unequivocal "no!".

Goggomobil, circa 1956.

micro-economics and mini-marts

In 1947, career military man George C Marshall put forward his four-year European Recovery Programme. Otherwise known as the Marshall Plan it was launched to increase economic integration, expand foreign trade and increase production. Regardless of the devastation wrought by the war, Marshall's investment was not aimed at infrastructural improvements—certainly no housing, schools or factories were budgeted for—but money was poured into economic superstructure, especially the energy sector and the heart of industrial dynamism: iron and steel.

American intervention was solely to strengthen the Deutschmark and revive German capitalists' shattered confidence by restoring adequate accumulation. Marshall's dollars, in Italy as in Germany, "symbolised wholehearted American support for this project. But their direct economic contribution was secondary."[12] Not exactly benign, there was nonetheless a massive boost to European domestic economies as a consequence. In one of the deals, the Ford Motor Company in the UK was offered monies to re-tool, so that they could increase production and earn foreign exchange credits. In four years, the US government spent nearly $12 billion, with $1.5 billion (approximately $70 and $15 billion dollars at current value) loans tied to strict repayment criteria: what Marshall had called 'friendly aid'. In Germany, in 1947, industrial production was just one third of what it had been before the war started. After four years of Marshall Aid, it was up to 1938 levels again and rising. Mostly, as some commentators have noted, this was because of economic 'reforms' foisted on the German state, rather than the straightforward benefits of direct aid and investment.

Goggomobil, circa 1955/1956.

Fritz Fend, the aeronautical design engineer who had worked on the German jet-engined Me262 Messerschmitt fighter aircraft, created his first car in 1947, within a few months of Marshall's speech. This pedal-powered "Flitzer" (meaning 'flitter') was pretty hopeless, resembling the doomed Sinclair C5 without the power, but his belief that he was minimising the use of essential materials and thus freeing them up for more useful purposes reflected the transient post war desperation for diversification. Fortunately, things were changing fast. The lack of real independence within economic policy and fiscal discipline had resulted in problems at the end of the war, with unemployment doubling to around 11 per cent. However, because of the mass influx of foreign aid directed towards manufacturing, industry still produced 25 per cent more goods, even with fewer workers. The start of the technologically driven boom was beginning. Low wages tended to be reflected in high profit margins, which meant that fewer external loans were required to finance the recovery. The German economic dynamic was being recreated and this was reflected in the way that Germany saw itself as a nation. The launch of the Deutschemark on 18 June 1947 was the start of what commentators called the "economic miracle and the rebirth of German ambition". Italy and Germany, the former pariah states, were eventually being allowed to develop. And so did two of the most recognisable names in microcar history: the Messerschmitt and Isetta. Both originated in countries where economies of scale and production efficiencies were essential. They had every incentive—sticks as well as carrots—to think big, but start small.

Epitomising this dictum, Fend, working with Willy Messerschmitt, produced the Messerschmitt KR175, launched in 1953. In the very clear references to an aeroplane's cockpit, with driver and passenger sitting tandem, they had adapted their experience of the aircraft industry and provided a cheap, small car with excellent road handling and the definitive shape that was celebrated in all future versions; suddenly, a vehicle represented the sense of the emergent Germany. Posters advertising "Fast, Reliable, Economical: The Incomparable Messerschmitt" summed it up and appealed to the new economic class. Owners of motorcycles, with or without sidecars were the target market as were people in their early twenties—those who had been young children during the war years. Across Europe, those who couldn't afford the Volkswagen, but still craved speedy mobility, bought the popular Messerschmitt models or the Heinkel. Just as they look curious now, so they looked curious back then. Desire for transport overcame any embarrassment—needs must. The Goggomobil meanwhile, was an attempt by Germany's Hans Glas to disguise the size by styling it to look like a proper car—a conceit somewhat undermined when an adult sat in it.

Italy and Germany, the former pariah states, were eventually being allowed to develop. And so did two of the most recognisable names in microcar history: the Messerschmitt and Isetta.

By the 1950s some people would purchase small cars and microcars simply to fulfil their undiminished ambition to drive....

In those days, there was a generally accepted belief that travel broadened the mind, fortunately so, because if you wanted to experience the open road in a microcar, you had to be fairly broad-minded to start with.

In Britain, the demands of the post war government to satisfy export markets meant that Britons were effectively driving around in pre war cars well into the late 1940s and beyond. "With the world's highest tax burden and the expensive Welfare State to sustain", said *Autocar* magazine, "existing small cars like the Morris Minor and Austin Seven are just as far out of reach of most people as cars of twice the engine size were before the war. Car ownership is ceasing to figure among the ordinary man's ambitions, and large numbers of people are faced with the prospect of giving up motoring when their present pre war cars wear out, unless an alternative is offered."[13]

Autocar was simply throwing down a rhetorical gauntlet. Even though research and design development in the UK hadn't been a high priority for the domestic market, there was still a massive unfulfilled need. The market for motorcycles was slumping, down from nearly 340,000 in 1952 to 160,000 three years later and so, by the 1950s some people would purchase small cars and microcars simply to fulfil their undiminished ambition to drive—to get their first step on the ladder to a larger and more credible motor car. Embodied in this act is the ambition that exemplifies the real struggle to achieve decent mobility, notwithstanding that people with greater purchasing power could possibly circumvent this stage. It is this very ambition which is strikingly at odds with the motoring ethos pertaining to small cars today, in a climate where we are frequently enjoined to reduce our car use.

The Second World War had been described as "the petrol war" referring to battle tactics that were premised on the development of "tracked vehicles, the use of outsized balloon tyres, and engines of ample power unfettered in design by any scruples as to horse-power tax or petrol consumption."[14] The motorised vehicle had come of age—whether with the General Purpose vehicle (Jeep) in the USA or with Hitler's Volkswagen, both were functional vehicles that exemplified the universal desire for personal mobility as well as the liberation that improved transportation could bring. In those days, there was a generally accepted belief that travel broadened the mind, fortunately so, because if you wanted to experience the open road in a microcar, you had to be fairly broad-minded to start with.

There had been many small car designs from the AC Petite to the Fiat 500, but there was a growing recognition that financial circumstances had created a demand that needed sating with more and better, designs dedicated to the microcar market. In Britain, the gearing of industry—and to a certain extent the fact that its manufacturing base and infrastructure hadn't been destroyed in the war—meant that it was more difficult for the big manufacturers to re-tool for reduced sizes in any great quantity. A lot of the market was being catered for by small manufacturers or localised kit-car entrepreneurs. Paradoxically, in the reconstruction of Germany, Italy and France there were more 'opportunities'.

BMW Isetta, 1959.

Heinkel's three-wheeler made its debut around the same time as the Messerschmitt KR200 in the mid-1950s; Heinkels were made under license in Dundalk on the border between southern and northern Ireland and, eventually, in Croydon, south London. Not exactly glamorous locations, but sufficiently industrious to make the car a success. *Autocar* described the British production model as being "about the lightest and smallest-engined vehicle offering standards of comfort, refinement and performance acceptable to owners of orthodox modern cars".[15] Manufactured at the Croydon plant from 1962 under license as the 'Trojan', over 6,000 were sold. By spring 1956, 16,000 KR200s came out of the Regensburg plant. Bearing in mind that in the early 1950s, only five million vehicles were on the road in Britain—compared to 30 million today—this was a sizeable market albeit spread over Europe.

A similar story pertained in Italy. The Isetta initially made by refrigerator manufacturer Iso lasted from 1953 until 1957, although deals in other countries meant that it remained in production, in Germany in particular, until 1964, selling some 160,000 units. The name, meaning 'little Iso' became known universally as the 'rolling egg' and was one of the principle reasons for the popularity of the appellation 'bubble car'. Its price, and 60mpg at 50mph capability, went down well with the desperate British buyers just entering Suez-inspired rationing. As importantly, the promotion of the 'maintenance-free' nature of the microcar was something for the poorer driver to factor in.

The name, meaning 'little Iso' became known universally as the 'rolling egg' and was one of the principle reasons for the popularity of the appellation 'bubble car'.

Japan had to wait to enter the microcar market with products like its 1958 Subaru 360. In post war Japan, management and unions alike were preoccupied with the rebuilding of Japan's economy. The so-called work ethic, as it was described in the West, masked the fact that "any independent trade union presence after these years was to be rapidly defeated by management with the assistance of the US occupying authority".[16] The reality however, was that severe hardship and the consequent hard-headed response to corporate employees was established with full Western complicity. 40 years later and American social scientist Francis Fukuyama cites the car industry as one where changes in production practices, particularly those lean manufacture issues that were brought to the attention of Western producers by Nissan and Toyota in the 1990s, came as a culture shock to the union-based car plants in Michigan. According to Fukuyama the impetus today for the advocacy of the rigours of lean manufacture and partnering is part of a general search for a romanticised Oriental social cohesion rising above consumerism, that can be applied to the West.[17]

Messerschmitt, late 1950s.

the political framework   The Macro World of Microcars

But back in the 1950s, consumption began to open up and foreign trade was being normalised. Even though British economic tribulations after the Marshall Plan were less severe than in continental Europe and Japan, with real wages around 28 per cent higher than in the immediate pre war period, spending power—or rather the real level of personal consumption—was just five per cent higher. In Japan, GDP grew at 10.5 per cent per annum for the next 20 years. Germany's GNP meanwhile grew from $32 billion in 1952 to $600 billion a decade later. Consumerism was being liberated.[18] Even though the 1950s was the period where the microcar flourished, they had definitely become an anachronism by the end of the decade given the pace of the social, cultural and political changes in the wider world. Elvis, the man who exemplified the transition from the 1950s to the 1960s, was definitely more bubblegum than bubblecar. There was more conspicuous consumption than cautious fuel consumption—more mess o'grits than Messerschmitts!

Reyner Banham writing at the end of the 1950s, referred to the decade as the First Machine Age. "Many technologies have contributed to (the) domestic revolution, but most of them make their point of impact on us in the form of small machines-shavers, clippers and hair dryers; radio, telephone, gramophone, tape recorder and television; mixers, grinders, automatic cookers, washing machines, refrigerators, vacuum cleaners, polishers." With the unprepossessing naiveté and boldness of the pre-politically correct age, he continued: "A housewife alone, often disposes of more horse-power today than an industrial worker did at the beginning of the century."[19] The microcar played a real technological and inventive function, but moreover, represented a new device to make life more pleasurable for those who wanted to leave the 1940s behind.

At the 1956 *Daily Mail* Ideal Home Exhibition, the *House of the Future,* designed by renowned architects Alison and Peter Smithson, was made of plastic and constructed so that it could be mass-produced. Glass reinforced plastic (GRP) was now regularly used in the construction of cars for its lightness, mouldability or simply because it was a sexy new material. With America conducting things from the wings, the visionary house even incorporated "such revolutionary features as a remote control for the TV".[20] Society wanted labour-saving devices combined with comfortable living standards and those that couldn't afford it had to resort to changing channels by throwing a slipper at the TV. It was a cheap, less attractive option, but at least it did the trick until you could afford the real deal. Societal aspirations for mobile comfort and convenience were being realised in the thriving small car market: the microcar was the drivable equivalent of the slipper.

"A housewife alone, often disposes of more horse-power today than an industrial worker did at the beginning of the century."
Reyner Banham

The microcar played a real technological and inventive function, but moreover, represented a new device to make life more pleasurable for those who wanted to leave the 1940s behind.

The microcar was the drivable equivalent of the slipper.

It was, in fact, a suitable solution to a very particular set of circumstances, satisfying a need for low-cost travel that would become an anachronism within the following decade. However, it's important not to fetishise the period too much. There were still real economic hardships that tended to hit all developed economies in different ways. America had taken its new found anti-communist message to the extreme and was waging war on Korea in an expensive flexing of its military muscle. In Britain the decade began with the Festival of Britain and ended with rationing, started with economic revival but finished with the Suez crisis.[21]

It was during this period that Sir Leonard Lord's dislike for the foreign importation of microcars and bubble cars caused him to demand of his chief engineer, Alec Issigonis to "drive them off the streets by designing a proper miniature car". If there's one enduring image of the following decade, it must surely be the Mini, launched for £496/$843 in May 1959. The minicar meant that the steady rise of the microcar was about to stall.

The winning car of the Rally Monte Carlo 1964: Paddy Hopkirk's Mini Cooper S ©BMW AG.

micro-economics and mini-marts   The Macro World of Microcars

the bubble bursts

The 1960s was a dynamic period of politicised youth, of protest, increased mobility, economic growth and investment. Roy Porter writes that at the time "corporations and governments worldwide were desperate to borrow capital, for financing expansion. Americans regarded London favourably; it was English-speaking and little regulated and it possessed financial experience".[22]

The British Prime Minister Harold Wilson conjured the can-do sense of socio-scientific progress with his speech on 'the white heat of technology'. Let's not get too carried away, though. America's first Western freeway, the Arroyo Seco Parkway had been built way back in 1940 carrying 27,000 cars a day, whereas in Britain the motorway building programme was still in its infancy by the mid-60s. But when UK Minister of Transport and Aviation, Ernest Marples MP, cut the ribbon on the M1 on 2 November 1959, the new breed of fast intra-urban travel caught the imagination.[23]

Motoring was in. So much so that Britain's Baron Beeching was able to launch his famous assault on Britain's railways in 1963, getting rid of steam (eliminating a massive cause of pollution at a stroke), slashing the useable length of passenger rails by a third and closing 2,128 stations. Beeching's forthrightness truly heralded the popular motor age. His government backed initiative was a real turn around from events in the past. Before the war, Marshall Stevens MP had complained that "road competition had been stunted by railway interests".[24] Just 45 years later, Beeching was happy to reverse that trend. Now, the car was the star. What did your car say about *you*? As styling became available to everyone, fewer and fewer people opted to drive around in a 1950s bubble.

Congestion in London 1969.

the bubble bursts   The Macro World of Microcars

The Gordon, built in Cheshire between 1954-1957 (by a subsidiary of Vernons Pools) was the cheapest car on the UK market. The Pools was a national institution, a working class tradition that meant that every Saturday afternoon, families would tick off their football scores and match them with James Alexander Gordon's sonorous intonation of the results. Vernons Pools instilled the Lottery mentality that there were possible riches to be had. Indeed, society was getting more wealthy—albeit imperceptibly to many working class people. The economy was picking up and this was reflected in the prices of commodities. The future seemed like a good place to be but Vernons seemed not to understand the contradiction: who would want to buy a 197cc single cylinder, two-stroke Villiers engine Gordon—one of the most unattractively 'designed' cars ever made, with its engine mounted on the off-side, and single rear-wheel chain drive—if they were hoping to win the Pools? Not many. By the end of the 1950s people were aspiring—and looking forward to being able to fulfil their aspirations—to bigger and better things.

Sean Topham describes the general mood of the 1960s as a time of unalloyed experimentation.[25] Designers were trying out new materials and shapes, industrial design was merging with domestic consumer products, and fashion was adapting to new technologies while challenging accepted norms. Things were moving rapidly and the *Futuro House*, designed by Finnish architect Matti Suuronen in the late 1960s was designed to reflect the spirit of the Space Age. Preformed out of 16 insulated GRP panels and with Perspex bug-eye windows it resembled a spaceship and was meant to emphasise the temporary, transient mobility of the age, but it had taken too long to get from prototype to finished product and it missed the moment. By the end of the 60s, the majority wanted bricks and mortar and fiscal certainties, not an experiment in yellow plastic. The sci-fi building, just like the microcar before it, was out of time. The changing face of history and the new social demands of consumers due to the expansion of efficient production methods meant that the time of mediated social mobility was over. No-one needed a small stepping stone to a decent family car; none wanted to stay in local authority housing stock; and nobody contented themselves with a black and white telly to watch *Pot Black*.[26] At last, ordinary desires for material improvements were actually achievable.

By the end of the 50s, the majority wanted bricks and mortar and fiscal certainties, not an experiment in yellow plastic.

Still from *Futuro—A New Stance for Tomorrow*, 1998, directed by Mika Taanila. Courtesy of Kinotar Productions.

The recognition of unlimited supplies of energy—a fact that remains as true today as it was then—is juxtaposed with the dawn of the Space Age and its exhilaration that distant planets were ours for the taking.

In 1960, Reyner Banham noted that, "our accession to almost unlimited supplies of energy is balanced against the possibility of making our planet uninhabitable". It is easy to pretend that this was ecological prescience on his part but he went on to say that, "this again is balanced, as we stand on the threshold of space, by the growing possibility of quitting our island earth and letting down roots elsewhere".[27] The recognition of unlimited supplies of energy—a fact that remains as true today as it was then—is juxtaposed with the dawn of the Space Age and its exhilaration that distant planets were ours for the taking. His aspiration for space was not premised on fleeing Earth as a defensive act, but rather adventuring into space as a positive exploratory act. Kennedy's famous speech in 1961 identified space exploration as "the most hazardous and dangerous and greatest adventure on which man has ever embarked".[28] At the turn of the 1960s, the sky, quite literally, was the limit. No wonder that the era had an inventive, dynamic, can-do, feel to it.

Wernher von Braun explains the Saturn Launch System to President John F Kennedy in 1963. Courtesy of NASA.

the bubble bursts   The Macro World of Microcars

By 1970, all but the most hard-bitten microcar owner and manufacturer had thrown in the towel. The remaining Bonds were curios; and the Reliants—before the rise of disability rights—had become a much-parodied vehicle for 'invalids' and for people who wore flat caps, had shiny plastic holdalls and drove at 15mph in odd socks. Microcars were dead. It seemed that the combined conditions of rationing, financial hardship and economic necessity that had brought on the microcar experiment had gone. Or had they?

In fact, in 1972 the oil crisis hit Europe hard and once again rationing ensued. *The Limits to Growth* was published, which argued that resources—predominantly oil—were running out and that we should stop exploiting natural materials at such a pace.[29] Pressure to reduce the reliance on non-renewables and to utilise the extant resource base more efficiently, was a major discussion primarily amongst policy-formers. In 1973, Schumacher published *Small is Beautiful* which proselytised the benefits of smallness and harmoniousness of local production.[30] M E Hoff of Intel Corporation had already managed to put all the logic circuitry on a chip the size of a fingernail.[31] Miniaturisation was carrying on apace. 'Small' was making a comeback. But with all the conditions seeming to mimic those of the 1950s when the original microcar came into its own (rationing, local production, miniature manufacture), the microcar died out altogether. The 'Save-It' campaign counselled frugality. The material conditions seemed to be right for the microcar to rise again, but instead everyone appeared to go for the big car option, going against the environmental grain.

This attitude suited the combative political climate of the 1970s that held sway throughout the West. This included a range of dramatic protests and radical trade union victories for satisfactory pay and conditions in Europe and America. The concept of the 'job-for-life' became a common expression and there reigned a stability of earnings that meant that the working classes were finally able to buy the objects of their desires. Americans had long had inset sinks, eye-level grilles and exercise machines, but now they were filtering into the affordable British range. Disposable incomes allowed people to buy calculators (£32/$54 in 1974) or enjoy themselves with Atari Pong! computer games (150,000 units sold in 1975). With such a positive, forward-thinking sentiment that exemplified the 1970s, it is little wonder that environmentalism was of marginal concern: talked about but seldom actioned. Material issues were the order of the day. Government campaigns to put a brick in your toilet cistern didn't have much resonance. While politicians talked of shortages, it was their problem, not ours.

But with all the conditions seeming to mimic those of the 1950s when the original microcar came into its own (rationing, local production, miniature manufacture), the microcar died out altogether.

Courtesy AR.

the bubble bursts   The Macro World of Microcars

Into the 1980s and the Thatcherite/Reaganite consumer revolution really kicked in. Margaret Thatcher's famous dictum that 'anyone over 30 who used buses was a failure' said it all.[32] Cars, cars and more cars. Mobile phones the size and weight of housebricks, Walkmans, microwaves, dishwashers, Brother computers, Betamax videos: this was the heyday of conspicuous consumption and microcars were anathema to the prevailing mood of 'more' (not less). City traders made fortunes and gave rise to lookalike bands such as Heaven 17, Spandau Ballet sang of "Gold!", the Yuppy was firmly ensconced in his warehouse conversion and all was right with the world. From the mid-80s onwards, BMW sales went up and up.[33] These were the status cars of the moment (and I don't mean Isettas). Big was beautiful.

microclimates

Throughout the 1960s, as a result of the developing road system in Britain, many a happy hour was spent by families parked on the hard shoulder of major arterial roads, with their picnic blankets spread out, chairs unfolded, happily munching on particulates washed down with sweet sulphurous tea. Carcinogens, PM10 and NOx, were unfamiliar concepts. Not only did motoring not cause obesity in those days, two sugars in your tea didn't seem to either. They were innocent times. Wills Wild Woodbine cigarettes ruled in the UK (with twice as many smokers then as today).[34] In America, Marlboro Country promoted their flavour. Filters were for cissies. Anyone that had come through the smogs of the early 1950s weren't put off by the mere whiff of traffic fumes. As London Mayor, Ken Livingstone says of the famous 1952 smog which is alleged to have killed almost 12,000 people:

> For those like me who were children at the time, its main impact was that we didn't have to go to school for a few days. The fog was simply so thick that parents were advised not to risk letting their children get lost on the way to school, unless it was literally round the corner. When my parents went out they had to cover their nose and mouth with a handkerchief.[35]

We were, it seems, more circumspect about pollution in the early days of motoring.

Courtesy AR.

Up until the late 1980s, environmental considerations were low down the priority list. Admittedly, things were not plain sailing. Pete Seeger had already droned about the anti-humanising effects of living in a commuter belt in 1963, and the 1970s kicked off with Joni Mitchell complaining about Big Yellow Taxis, closely followed by the Osmonds imploring us, in 1972, to "stop them crazy horses". Fortunately, the combined forces of folk music and Osmania couldn't change our positive attitude to the car. While governments were unabashedly engaged in a massive road-building programme, the issue of car exhausts seemed churlish.[36] Conversely, today, almost the entire transport debate is taken up by consideration of air, noise or visual pollution. Working out how best to get from A to B is pretty low down the list of transport priorities. As we have seen, concern for the environment is nothing new, so what changed and why did cars start to shrink in response?

It was in 1987 that Gro Harlem Brundtland, Norwegian Prime Minister and Chair of the World Commission of Environment and Development, launched her salvo against what she perceived to be unsustainable development, a concept that says that we should minimise the risk from actions that might subsequently be shown to be harmful to future generations.[37] This sentiment of anticipatory precaution finds expression in a fundamental loss of nerve in experimentation and change—everything that symbolised the heyday of the microcar—and its demise. Given that a Bond Bug might roll at speed, or that a Scootacar didn't come with an excess of safety features, if the precautionary principle had applied in the past, the microcar might never have seen the light of day.

Working out how best to get from A to B is pretty low down the list of transport priorities.

Courtesy AR.

By the start of the 1990s, consumerism and growth were becoming *passé*.[38] Big was not only not beautiful, it was deemed to be unsustainable. The Commission on Global Governance had a blunt message for all: "Environmental sustainability", it said, "requires restraint on consumption at a global level".[39] This period corresponded with a sense of political uncertainty after 1989 and renewed professions of faith in market forces were not enough. Even hard-nosed establishment commentators were longing for ideological security and 'the environment' became the most socially cohering idea on offer.[40] So much so that even Thatcher tried to buy into the new eco-moment and address the 'vexed' issue of pollution.

The new generation of microcars, which range from Nissan's Urban Rental System to Toyota's Crayon[41] project; from Norway's Th!nk[42] to Honda's Mon Pal[43], try to outdo the other in prioritising their minimal—rather than maximum—impact on the environment. So much so, that few people will have heard of them! We've moved from the 1950s microcar as a dynamic and inventive response to a demand for increased physical, as well as fiscal and social mobility, to a situation whereby today's microcars are more often than not, symbolic of a *renunciation* of that demand.[44]

The contemporary enthusiasm for road tolling, from Dublin to Toronto to Trondheim accepts the principle that there is not enough space so there needs to be a reduction in the footprint of motor vehicles. London's congestion charge dissuades people from entering the inner city area by charging them five pounds in order to reduce the amount of traffic in the central area of the city. Scooters and electric vehicles are currently exempted from paying—presaging a secondary burst of interest in micro-vehicles.

However, the number of car movements in central London is exactly the same as it was in the mid-1960s which tends to suggest that we have either become over-sensitised to congestion, or, that the constriction of road space has squeezed smaller and smaller cars into smaller and smaller spaces.

Renowned futurologist Peter Schwartz is one of the few upbeat voices commenting about future societal trends when he says that "some solution to the gridlock problem is inevitable. We don't know when it will occur, or where it will happen first, but we know that places with well-designed transit and traffic infrastructure will thrive."[45] His sentiments are notable for their dissonance with commonly held beliefs that gridlock can never be alleviated by infrastructural measures. Cities affected by the march towards reducing their vehicular access include Barcelona, Lyon, Freiburg, Copenhagen, Cordoba and Strasbourg and the demand for similar responses across the rest of Europe is increasing. The idea, it seems, is to 'reclaim' public space from private vehicles. Obviously, as major manufacturing plants continue to produce ever more cars, the tension of the situation is becoming palpable.

It would be crazy to suggest that car-based traffic has had its day, but in contradistinction to a time when everyone from Nat King Cole to Jackie Trent and Tony Hatch could immortalise a road in song—albeit a 2,400 mile-long transnational Route 66 completed in the 1930s—cars today are seen by many as the predominant problem, representative not of freedom, but of restriction.[46] In this context, the modern microcar is less a celebration of motorised liberation, but a guilty apology for mobility *per se*. Marina Benjamin, author of *Rocket Dreams*, yearns for that ideal of "contact and communion, a quest for new horizons and frontiers; for human expansion and even for salvation".[47] Unfortunately, the late 1950s and 1960s have gone and the desperate clamour for certainties says more about our time than anything else. Today, in the West, we view the future with trepidation instead of anticipation, and universal solutions are derided in favour of individualistic responses. The new generation of microcar, city car or small car is the response to that sense of loss and longing—a reflection of parochial values. Car clubs are springing up all over the place to give a sense of a shared experience and both governments and businesses are enjoining people to take up multiple occupancy (a glorified minibus service) to try to ferment social interaction. In South Africa, there was even a government report unabashedly entitled 'Translating Social Policy into Transport Regulation'.[48]

Thankfully, there are still innovative technologies and creative designs around—but even small production runs typical of kit car and microcar production has a certain sense of a renunciation of modern labour efficiencies that have evolved over many years. Small production of small cars is becoming a growing niche market but is the polar opposite to the positive rise of microcars in the 1950s. It is a fairly deft slap in the face of Fordism, too.

"... some solution to the gridlock problem is inevitable. We don't know when it will occur, or where it will happen first, but we know that places with well-designed transit and traffic infrastructure will thrive."
Peter Schwartz

The new generation of microcar, city car or small car is the response to that sense of loss and longing— a reflection of parochial values.

But for a sense of developmental dynamism, look no further than the emerging economic nations. An Indonesian aircraft manufacturer, PT Dirgantara is developing a microcar, or 'imut-imut' (translated as 'small and cute'), which at 6ft x 3ft x 4ft high and with a fibreglass-reinforced plastic shell will have a fuel efficiency of 112mpg. California's XCORP's microcar, the VirtualCar, incorporating poly-metal matrix composite components is also intended for Eastern Europe, China and India. However, we need only examine the situation on the Indian sub-continent for a fast-forward replay of the 1960s Western sense of emerging affluence. "Ford and Chrysler tried to bring in a sub-Rs 2 lakh (200,000 rupees) but they were laughed out of car clinics in India", says Hormazd Sorabjee of *Autocar India*. "Eicher and Kinetic with their microcars—which looked more like glorified golfcarts—experienced a similar consumer response. The problem is that producing an econo-car less than a Maruti 800 is considered too minimalistic. The 800 has become the benchmark for what an entry-level car should be—the first step from two wheels to four."[49] Anyone who bought a Heinkel in the post war years will understand what he means. Meanwhile, the other side of microcar technology can be seen in Japan, where a 1/1000th scale Toyota 1936 AA sedan was built in 1995. A true microcar, it is the size of a grain of rice and is a fully motorised working model demonstrating micro-precision engineering and ultimately displaying the potential for nano-technologies to come. Technologies such as drive-by-wire, coming on stream in a few years time, will undoubtedly further reduce the physical space required for erstwhile mechanical connections currently cluttering up our bonnets, and drive the progression of efficiencies of scale. Even Dean Kamen's Sinclair-esque Segway™ Human Transporter with its ingenious Dynamic Stabilisation will undeniably come good, hopefully achieving as Bill Machrone of *PC Magazine* says, "a significant technology trickle-down over the next few years".[50] Here's hoping.

In Japan a 1/1000th scale Toyota 1936 AA sedan was built in 1995. It is the size of a grain of rice and is a fully motorised working model demonstrating micro-precision engineering and ultimately displaying the potential for nano-technologies to come.

A 1936 Toyota AA Sedan at a 1:1000 scale. ©Denson Corporation.

So looking back at the pioneering golden age of the microcar should give us cause to reflect on what's missing in the current debate. The modern microcar in the West exists purely and simply because it is small—in every respect. The original microcars however existed because they had pretentions to be big. Nevertheless, microcar manufacturers shouldn't lose their faith. As Daniel Howes states in the *Detroit News*: "A joint venture with Toyota to develop and build (most likely in Poland) a cost-effective microcar for developing markets recognises both the need to play in a segment that promises long-term growth and to have a rich, strong partner."[51] So it seems that the rise and rise of the modern microcar in the East will continue for as long as they have unfulfilled ambition. In the West, the modern microcar will continue as long as social concerns—separate to issues of mobility, speed and convenience—are given priority in transport debates. Unfortunately, it looks as if both conditions will be the case for a good while yet.

The modern microcar in the West exists purely and simply because it is small—in every respect. The original microcars however existed because they had pretentions to be big.

The Segway™.

endnotes

1 Setright, LKJ, *Drive On! A Social History of the Motor Car*, London and New York: Granta Publications, 2003, p. 89.

2 Pries, Ludger, "The Volkswagen in the 1990s: Accelerating from a Multinational to a Transnational Automobil Company", in *Globalization or Regionalization of the European Car Industry?*, eds. Freyssenet, Michel, Shimizu, Koichi and Volpato, Giuseppe, Basingstoke and New York: Palgrave Macmillan, 2003.

3 Between 1971-1976, sales of the Volkswagen Type 1 slumped by 92 per cent in the US and for a long time, Volkswagen was unable to rekindle similar excitement in its models in order to recoup the lost sales volumes.

4 *Kraft durch Freunde* ('Power through Friends'), also called the *KdF*, was one of the most popular organisations of the Nazi era, leading the Volkswagen project and organising activities for workers such as collective holidays. Their aim was to boost production and therefore armaments while maintaining low wages.

5 The shift towards more intelligent kid's comics in Britain was typified by *The Eagle* edited by Reverend Marcus Morris which put the fortitude of Dan Dare centre stage. This was Britain with a new moral agenda and an American chin.

6 The Avengers episode *The Girl from Auntie*, 1966. 15 years after it first began manufacture, the appearance of the micro (registration 505 TPU) was for comic effect only.

7 Kennedy, Paul, *The Rise and Fall of the Great Powers: Economic Change and Military Conflict From 1500 To 2000*, London: Fontana Press, 1988, p. 494.

8 Rader, James, *Penetrating the U.S. Auto Market: German and Japanese Strategies 1965-1976*, Ann Arbor, MI: UMI Research Press, 1980, p. 3.

9 Kenney, Martin and Florida, Richard, *Beyond Mass Production: The Japanese System and its Transfer to the US*, Oxford: Oxford University Press, 1993, p. 301.

10 quoted in Faith, Nicholas, *Crash: The Limits of Car Safety*, London: Boxtree, 1997, p. 25.

11 Henry Ford, 1946, quoted in "The Problem of Thinking Small", *Forbes Magazine*, Flint, Jerry, 20 May 2003.

12 Armstrong, Philip, Glyn, Andrew and Harrison, John, *Capitalism Since 1945*, Oxford: Blackwell, 1991, p. 94.

13 "How Much Can You Do Without?" (*Autocar*, 5 September 1952) cited in *Road Tests & Articles, Microcars Volume 3*, ed. Trevor Alder, London: Transport Source Books, 1993.

14 Buchanan, C D, *Mixed Blessings: The Motor in Britain*, London: Leonard Hill Books Ltd, 1958, p. 16.

15 "The Heinkel Cabin Cruiser" in Alder, *Road Tests*, p. 31.

16 Garrahan, Philip and Stewart, Paul, *The Nissan Enigma: Flexibility at Work in a Local Economy*, London: Mansell, 1992, p. 10.

17 Fukuyama, Francis, *The Great Disruption: Human Nature and the Reconstitution of Social Order*, London: Profile Books, 1999, p. 222.

18 Kennedy, *Rise*, pp. 539-550.

19 Banham, Reyner, *Theory and Design in the First Machine Age*, London: Architectural Press, 1960, p. 10.

20 Shinn, Matt, "Hype or home-makers?", *The Architects' Journal*, 22 January 2004, p. 53.

21 Petrol rationing was reintroduced in the UK after Suez with each private motorists being allowed an allocation of 10 gallons each month.

22 Porter, Roy, *London: A Social History*, London: Penguin, 1994, p. 459.

23 In fact, built in 1958, the 8.26 miles from Broughton in the north to Bamber Bridge, known as the Preston bypass was the first motorway in Britain.

24 quoted in Thorold, Peter, *The Motoring Age: The Automobile and Britain 1896-1939*, London: Profile Books, 2003, p. 171.

25 Topham, Sean, *Where's My Space Age: The Rise And Fall of Futuristic Design*, Munich and New York: Prestel, 2003.

26 *Pot Black* was the first colour broadcast (BBC2). A televised snooker game it was first broadcast in July 1969 and helped increase the sales of colour sets.

27 Banham, *Theory*, p. 9.

28 Public Papers of the Presidents of the United States, v. 1, 1962, pp. 669-670.

29 Meadows, Donella H et al, eds. *The Limits to Growth: A report for the Club of Rome's Project on the Predicament of Mankind*, London: Macmillan, 1974.

30 Schumacher, E F, *Small is Beautiful: Study of Economics as if People Mattered*, London: Vintage, 1993.

31 20 years earlier, in 1950, a typical computer contained 4,000 tubes, six miles of wire and 100,000 soldered joints, cost half a million pounds and used 30,000 watts of power to run.

32 cited in Clark, Andrew, "On (and off) the buses", *The Guardian*, 13 November 2003.

33 In 1991, BMW U.S. sales dropped to 53,343 from a high just five years earlier of 96,759' from Roemer, Bob, "The BMW Century", *The Roundel*, BMW Car Club of America, January 2002.

34 In the States, cigarette consumption peaked in 1961 with 3986 cigarettes consumed per capita per annum and, unlike some, most inhaled.

35 Ken Livingstone quoted in "Fifty Years On: The Struggle for Air Quality in London since the Great Smog of December 1952", Greater London Authority, 2002.

36 The European Community Directive on the mandatory use of three-way catalytic converters was introduced in 1993.

37 Sustainable development is "development that meets the needs of the present without compromising the ability of future generations to meet their own needs". *Our Common Future: From One Earth to One World*, World Commission on Environment and Development, Oxford: Oxford University Press, 1987.

38 "In 1988 and 1989 there was a great burst of public interest in the environment... however, the environmental lobby used the concern about global warming to attack capitalism, growth and industry". Thatcher, Margaret, *The Downing Street Years*, London: Harper Collins, 1993, p. 638.

39 *Our Global Neighbourhood: The Report of The Commission on Global Governance*, Oxford: Oxford University Press, 1995, p. 145.

40 'Ecological thinking' as it was sometimes called in those days, was seen as being able to "recover the very idea of a radical idea of social life". See Bookchin, Murray, "Toward An Ecological Society", Montréal and Buffalo: Black Rose Books, 1980.

41 Crayon is "a sophisticated communications and control system. Crayon allows 300 users to share 50 Toyota e-coms for commuting between the workplace and train stations, as well as for short trips around Toyota City. Crayon's real-time technology includes wireless central tracking of each car's location and charge, keyless access using smart cards, and web-based vehicle reservations. The project is exploring how to make car sharing more convenient and usable, in addition to the benefits of reduced traffic congestion and lower air pollution." See www.toyota.com

42 See www.think.no

43 Honda's proposed ICVS (Intelligent Community Vehicle System) is a "limited range transportation system for the near future in which system members share environment-friendly vehicles, such as small electric cars and electric-power assisted bicycles". See world.honda.com

44 "Nothing dates faster than the future, yet it is the nostalgic visions of the future which are fuelling some of the most interesting modern designs. It is a new kind of retro-futuristic historicism." See Heathcote, Edwin, "Sci-Fi Modernism and Space-Age Retro" in *Architectural Design*, ed Rachel Armstrong, Indianapolis, IN: Wiley-Academy, 2000, p. 77.

45 Schwartz, Peter, *Inevitable Surprises: A Survival Guide fro the 21st Century*, London: Free Press, 2003, p. 88.

46 Britain has just 2,245 miles of motorways nationally. At the turn of the millennium, the USA boasted 3.9 million miles of public road network.

47 Benjamin, Marina, *Rocket Dreams: How the Space Age Shaped Our Vision of a World Beyond*, London: Vintage, 2004.

48 "Moving South Africa: Translating Social Policy into Transport Regulation", Department of Transport. A presentation at the Transport Forum 2000 for the World Bank Group.

49 Sorabjee, Hormazd, *Autocar India*, editorial, April 2002. See www.autocarindia.com.

50 Machrone, Bill, "Segue: From Ginger to Segway", *PC Magazine*, 9 January 2002.

51 Howes, Daniel, "Peugeot-Citroën gains strength in Europe as its rivals founder", *The Detroit News*, 16 October 2001.

Chapter Two

The Contemporary Culture Of Microcars

the contemporary culture of microcars

Working on this book, it didn't take long before stories began to emerge of microcars being pelted with eggs, set on fire, rolled down hills by gangs of scornful youths.

From design cognoscenti to long-term, committed owners, collectors with fulsome chequebooks to those with minimal resources but maximum passion, a small but dedicated group of people has long understood that microcars have a value unseen by many. But what is it about these cars that causes them to be so undervalued, that attracts wide-spread contempt, despite their large numbers (and there were thousands of them on the roads during the 1940s and 50s), despite their doggedly aspirational character (which saw them address crisis after crisis from fuel to material shortages while bringing mobility to the masses after World War Two)? Working on this book, it didn't take long before stories began to emerge of microcars being pelted with eggs, set on fire, rolled down hills by gangs of scornful youths. Why was the point so badly missed? And just where did these cars end up? Apocryphal stories abound: are there really 80 Frisky car bodies under the A20 or Nobels under the A12 roads?

Isetta, late 1950s.

ROMI—the Brazilian version of the Isetta.

While most of these stories remain unsubstantiated—the stuff of speculation and conjecture—they reveal a deeply rooted fascination amongst the owners and those who take an interest in these tiny vehicles. Moreover, the paucity of formal documentation on microcars—itself an indication of their status as poor relation to 'proper' cars—has rendered personal anecdotes and testimonies crucial elements of the cars' history. Stories of commercial and personal endeavours can aptly describe the particular identities and idiosyncrasies of both, owners and automobile. In fact, they make up part of the overall historical value of each car and are therefore being collected and cherished conscientiously. Collectors are usually aware of who designed, engineered, funded and owned their particular vehicles. This stands in stark contrast to the majority of mass produced 'conventional' cars of today whose production process stays anonymous and universal. Owner after owner tells a similar story of how they or their families first came upon the cars, most often because they needed transport and, for a variety of reasons, a 'proper' car was out of reach. Initially, post war waiting lists for cars together with relatively high prices (both in terms of purchase and running costs) led potential buyers towards the option of a motorcycle—with or without sidecar—or scooter. Taxation laws meant that a three-wheeler, with no reverse gear, could be taxed for the same price as a motorcycle.[1] Also, many people had passed their motorcycle test but were yet to get car licenses. As a result, the microcar offered motorcycle license-holders a reasonable alternative to a pre war or second hand car. While some bought them as an additional family car—either for 'the wife' or for the offspring— a great deal of people acquired a microcar as their only vehicle.

There are three 'types' of ownership in the microcar's relatively short history: those who bought them 'the first time round', when they initially appeared on the market; those who acquired them— both new and used—for economic motoring during a period of revived popularity in the 1960s and 1970s; and a range of contemporary owners—those who initially got the cars as a means of transport but have turned collectors, or others, who, after having become interested in the history of the microcar, started collecting from scratch. A fourth category of buyers is now emerging: those who are driving the new version of the 'microcar' of which the Smart is, for the moment, the best known example. These owners—environmentally-aware and open to innovation—may know little about the forerunners to the small car and see it as one solution to the demands of twenty-first century motoring.

Goggomobil, circa 1956.

"After the end of War, it was hard to actually buy a car. There was a waiting list for, say, a Ford 8. All that was really available was either a motorcycle or a scooter. So there was a great market for these little cars. They were a step up from the rain and the weather and, by the standards of the time, the cars were exciting." Jean Hammond

Was it their lack of a fourth wheel or their size that led to them being treated as quirky, seldom taken seriously—at best dismissed and, at worst, ridiculed, destined never to be seen as 'proper' cars? Were their remarkable aspirations ahead of their time? Microcar manufacture was basic to say the least—some of their Space Age-looks belied technology that could not deliver. Frankly, travelling any real distance on anything less than perfect terrain was no joy. But many of them incorporated innovative and creative solutions challenging the difficulties of producing new, economical, lightweight, small cars. These cars laid the groundwork for the Mini and, on its appearance, they were unceremoniously dumped for a 'better' model of small car.

There are many lessons to be learned from microcars. With a century of motoring only a mere blip on the historical horizon, and with the jury still out on the next developmental stage in motoring, a renewed look at these cars can only be beneficial. The owners' clubs and rallies are populated with committed, enthusiastic and knowledgeable owners. The rest of the automotive and design world has much to learn from them.

Messerschmitt.

the contemporary culture of microcars   The Macro World of Microcars

owners and clubs

The microcar phenomenon is truly international, with owners clubs all over the world from the United States and Canada to Japan, Australia and New Zealand, Brazil, Uruguay, Argentina and across Europe, with contacts and affiliations between them. One of the activities common to the majority of owners clubs is the 'rally'—a more or less annual event at which owners gather with their cars to award prizes, compare notes, swap experiences and generally socialise. Many of the rallies began because car owners needed advice on a particular maintenance job or a certain part that might be hard to find. Today, members still gather at rallies to discuss their cars and drive in *concours d'elegance* much to the joy and puzzlement of passers-by. Most clubs have a magazine or a newsletter and, increasingly, the internet provides the forum for exchanges of information. The membership of clubs ranges from single model owners to those in which engine size is the criteria (usually vehicles with engines under 700cc), to clubs that cover a geographical area. The spectrum of microcars encompasses those more commonly recognisable to the non-expert (for example, the Isettas, Messerschmitts, Heinkels and Bonds), as well as those less well known outside the microcar circuit but important within it (the Goggomobils and Friskys) and those that were only ever produced in very small numbers or never made it into the wider public consciousness.

Members gather at rallies to discuss their cars and drive in 'concours d'elegance' much to the joy and puzzlement of passers-by.

BMW Isetta, circa 1957.

Goggomobil Van.

Heinkel.

In the UK, the first rally for more than one make of microcar was the Multi-make Three-Wheeler Rally held in 1974. The event became the key annual meeting point for many owners and spawned a whole host of rallies around the UK. Still referred to by owners generically as "Burford", long after it stopped being held there, the National Microcar Rally now happens at different UK locations each year, with owners bringing their cars by road and transporter from all around the United Kingdom, Europe and occasionally beyond.

Tony Marshall, long-time member of the microcar fraternity, tells the story of how the first Burford rally came about:

"We didn't know what we were getting into, how many cars there were or how many would turn up. The first one in 1974 happened with help from members of the Messerschmitt Owners Club. What is now called the Bond Owners Club already existed and came along en masse, assembling at the gates of the park and arriving in convoy. There was the Messerschmitt Enthusiasts Club and the Berkeley Enthusiasts Club. As a result of the early Burford rallies, the Isetta Owners Club started, then the Heinkel Trojan Club, as well as a lot of regional clubs in the UK. They all run their own events. The format of the rallies is similar now, not just in the UK but all over the world: Germany, Holland, Spain, Austria and Scandinavia, the States, Australia and New Zealand. The 2004 National Microcar Rally will be the 30th in the UK."

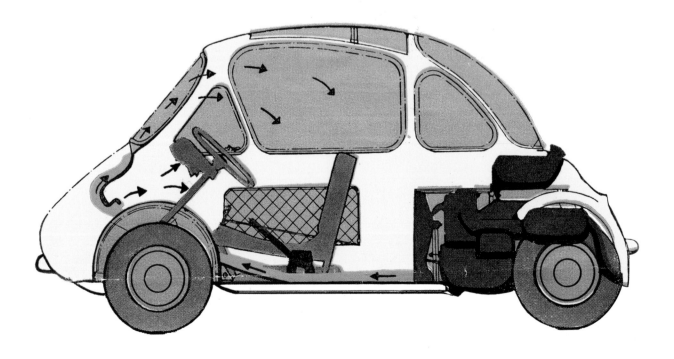

record breakers

Whilst the assumption may be that these cars were used only locally, many owners clocked up hundreds of miles, using their cars for both business and pleasure. As an extension of this, many acts of derring-do and feats of skill and endurance have taken place over the years to demonstrate the capabilities and durability of the cars—an evolution of the tests that these and other, more conventional cars, go through on 'proving grounds'. Contemporary microcar owners continue to uphold the tradition, completing long and often arduous journeys. Whereas ownership of a new car—large or small—is usually determined by a desire for trouble-free motoring, ownership of a microcar comes with a certain level of risk and a range of contingencies. Owners often need a degree of mechanical expertise as well as a readiness for experimentation. Drivers often develop their own methods of handling their particular cars to take account of their idiosyncrasies:

"A special driving technique had to be learned for driving the Bond. The camber of the road exerted a great pull on the engine, which was mounted on the single front wheel, causing a permanent pull to the left. This had to be compensated for by the driver adopting a 'quarter past two' hand position on the steering wheel. Also, the single cylinder engine had a tendency to stall at low revolutions so a technique of 'toeing and heeling' on the brake and throttle pedals had to be learned—similar to that used by racing drivers—to prevent stalling while braking. All Bond drivers that I met confessed to using this system."[2]

For safe Reliable & Economical Motoring Buy the **Bond Minicar** MARK 'C'

● 85-90 M.P.G. 50 M.P.H.
● Less than 1d per mile. (in spite of petrol price increase.)
● TAX Only £5 per annum.

Prices from £268 (inc. p. tax).

The World's Cheapest Motoring

SHARPS COMMERCIALS LTD., PRESTON ENGLAND.

For nearly three decades, one key rally destination was the Automuseum Störy, south of Hanover in Germany, run by Otto and Marianne Künnecke. Owners and their cars from all over Europe and beyond have made long journeys to gather there at the *Kleinwagentreffen* ("microcar meeting"), an annual rally held at the Museum since 1975. The last rally was in 2002 but visitors still travel from far and wide to see the collection which includes 140 cars from the AC Petite to the Zündapp Janus, and 140 motorcycles, scooters and mopeds.

Rally at Automuseum Störy, circa 1988.

In 1954, a Bond Minicar Mark C was unofficially entered into that year's Monte Carlo Rally by two army officers, Lieutenant Colonel M Crosby and Captain T Mills. It took three and a half days to travel the 2,000 miles (3,200 km) from Glasgow to Monte Carlo.[3]

In 1959, Douglas Ferreira covered the 873 miles from Land's End to John O'Groats in a Bond Minicar Mark F in less than 24 hours, at just over 36mph and 60mpg. Marketing at the time majored on this achievement, promoting the car's ability to cost "1d [1 penny] per mile, emphasising yet again the comfort, reliability and economy of Britain's most popular three-wheeler".

Shortly after it was launched in 1962, a Reliant 3/25 drove almost 2,500 miles from Birmingham to Oslo in 1962 and then, through the south of Scandinavia, to Rotterdam, from where they were flown back to London. The car achieved 58.1mpg.

collectors and collecting

Concerns about authenticity are as prevalent and vigorous in the microcar world as in any collecting community and numerous rumours circulate about the genuineness of specific cars. Ageing cars in poor states of repair are still being found, while parts are becoming increasingly scarce. Buying one car in a reasonable condition, and a second one to be used for parts, is a common practice amongst owners. A popular alternative is to restore cars with replica parts made out of new materials. There is almost an unspoken code of conduct amongst the long-standing owners that any use of replica parts, or adaptation of parts from one vehicle to another, should be made explicit.

There are a number of motives for buying or collecting in the microcar fraternity but probably one of the most powerful is a desire to preserve and keep these cars before their inevitable deterioration renders them un-salvageable. While some microcars including the Isetta, Goggomobil and Bond were produced in their thousands, it is questionable how many makes were manufactured in anything approaching mass production. Many of the clubs and registers are engaged in trying to track down 'lost' cars and the pleasure, when a previously unknown car is added to a register, is great. Equally powerful is the concern about the disappearance of cars–by being sold they sometimes become separated from any documentation or personal knowledge that once went with individual cars.

In the UK, the Register of Unusual Microcars is run by Jean Hammond. Jean, and her late husband Edwin, became involved in the microcar world when looking for a means of transport other than a motorbike for their son, Andrew. Searching for an affordable alternative lead them to a Heinkel.

Many of the clubs and registers are engaged in trying to track down 'lost' cars and the pleasure, when a previously unknown car is added to a register, is great.

"In 1976, my son Andrew was about 14 and wanted a motorbike. I was petrified of them so my husband decided that he and Andrew would restore a car. He didn't tell him what sort and, when it came, it was a blue Heinkel. We got it from a student in Brighton." Jean Hammond

"Thursday was Exchange and Mart day!"

Searching for parts in *Exchange and Mart*, the best source for microcar parts in the United Kingdom at the time, they came across an advert for the National Microcar Rally and went along to source spare parts for the reconditioning of their Heinkel. They found that the microcar was not only an affordable means of transport, but that it brought with it an entire community of enthusiasts. Jean and Edwin went on to collect a wide range of microcars and set up the Register of Unusual Microcars for owners of microcars without their own dedicated club (and engine sizes under 700cc). Today there are over 1,000 cars on the register and more coming to light every day. Jean also spends time putting TV researchers and the motoring press in touch with owners and is unflinching in her belief that "microcars are not just figures of fun but a very special part of motoring history."[4]

Though small in car ownership terms, the microcar fraternity itself is broad, from collectors who doggedly drive their vehicles on the road, to those who insist on maintaining the quality of their cars by transporting them to each show and rally on the back of a truck. In 1997 an auction run by London auction house Christie's marked the start of a new phase in the collecting of microcars: Bruce Weiner, American microcar collector and bubble gum king, sold his collection. The auction had a significant amount of advance publicity and microcar owners and classic car collectors flocked to Jack Barclay's showroom in South London on the day. Prices shocked and surprised everyone and "even caused the most dedicated of microcar enthusiasts present to gasp in amazement".[5]

Motor car comfort at motor cycle cost

Bond Minicar Mark C, circa 1952.

"Lots of people used these cars for their day-to-day transport. There were people who had their car from the beginning and never had anything else. Then the Mini came in and people stopped buying them. That's why we were able to buy the cars we did in the late 1970s and 1980s because people just didn't want them anymore. They would ask us to take them away."
Jean Hammond

1964 Peel Trident

Reserve price:
£3,000-5,000/$5,100-8,500

Sold for:
£25,000/$42,500

1959 Goggomobil TL400 (van)

Reserve price:
£7,000-9,000/$11,000-15,300

Sold for:
£19,000/$32,300

All images © Beaulieu Motor Museum, England.

Feelings amongst microcar owners about the impact of the auction vary. That so many of the cars ended up in the hands of private collectors with bulging wallets was a sad turn of events to some who had been collecting the cars for decades, often travelling miles to salvage a microcar that none else wanted. The injection of cash was short-lived though prices never returned to pre auction levels. The auction itself remains a key event in recent microcar history and its merits, or otherwise, are still hotly debated. Some feel that, as a result of the auction, collecting microcars became a chequebook hobby, shifting priorities so that the cars became objects invested with a previously unseen financial value rather than a personal or historical one. Others see the auction as having had a positive effect, raising the profile of the remaining un-restored cars which are, as a result still being rescued. It also encouraged collectors old and new to preserve the cars and, where possible, to exhibit them publicly.

The major motor museums have few microcars in their collections, and those individuals with significant collections find it hard to convince funders and publishers of their worth, preferring to single-mindedly develop their collections and show them to those who express an interest. Just how to ensure that these vehicles are given the value and status they deserve without inflating prices is a challenge.

The People

A selection of the **microcar owners** and collectors, and the events that have taken place around them. Whilst there are similarities across the stories, every one is individual; combined, they go some way to explaining the **microcar world**.

Accompanying photographs are by David Cowlard unless otherwise stated.

Lane Motor Museum
Nashville, Tennessee, USA

Opened in November 2003, the Lane Motor Museum in Tennessee shows a collection of European cars, which includes a Peel Trident, a Nobel, Scootacars Mark 1 and 2, Fiat 500, Reliant Regal and Berkeley, as well as a Subaru 360 and Crosley Hot Shot. As a boy, Jeff Lane was introduced to European cars when his father brought back an MGTF from Germany. Jeff passed his driving test in an MGTF and his move into microcars came via an interest in Citroën. Jeff drives his cars locally. Visitors to the Museum come from far and wide.

Lane Motor Museum. Photos: David Yando.

Bob Bareham
and his Bond Minicar

"I had neither the cash nor the inclination to join the 'ton up' boys on their Vincents, Triumphs and BSAs and, in 1962, passed my test on a 98cc James Comet and never rode a bike again. Instead, I chose the questionable luxury of a microcar...."

"I had neither the cash nor the inclination to join the 'ton up' boys on their Vincents, Triumphs and BSAs and, in 1962, passed my test on a 98cc James Comet and never rode a bike again. Instead, I chose the questionable luxury of a microcar, which could be driven with only a motorbike license as long as it had no reverse. For £25/$43 I became the proud owner of a 1953 Bond Minicar Mark C. My first outing was my first date with my (now) wife. She only discovered later that the journey was my first time on the road in anything that didn't have two wheels and handlebars."

"I started to commute about 60 miles a day round the South Circular Road to college so I decided to upgrade. I sold the Mark C for £27/$48 and bought a 1959 Mark F for £120/$204—most of which I had to borrow from my parents. The Mark F was a quantum leap in my motoring—doors on both sides, a hard top, proper lights, indicators and, most exciting of all, an electric starter. Engaged by now, my fiancée and I used to travel in the Bond to visit her family who, at that time, lived in and around Redcar on the north east coast. My future in-laws had no car of their own so the Mark F did many journeys carrying all sorts of large and awkward objects between Kent and Teeside. Most of these journeys were made at night—I would pick up my future wife from her office in the Strand and we'd drive north through the centre of London. The average journey time was seven to eight hours and we must have stopped in nearly every lay-by on the old A1. We got married in 1966 and travelled to Bournemouth in the Mark F for our honeymoon."

"After about six years of microcars and, having passed the full test, we sold the Mark F and went to four wheels. It would be about then that the effect of the introduction of the Austin/Morris Mini hit the demand for micros and only the older drivers with only a motorbike licence carried on using them."

This photograph was taken in 1965 after one of Bob's epic journeys north. The badges on the car are (from left to right):
North Kent Bond Owners Club, The National Bond Owners Club and the Elliott Motor Club.

Ray totally re-built this 250cc Mark G Estate which came third in the 2003 National Microcar Rally.

Ray Glendinning and his Bond Minicars

Ray Glendinning, rally co-ordinator for the Micromaniacs Club, first came across this Bond Mark E Tourer (left) when one of his sons asked if a friend could keep a three-wheeler in his garage.

"It was in need of a total restoration. I found out from the Bond Owners Club that it was a Mark E, and only the sixth to be known about at the time by the Club. Apparently, it was on the club register some years previously but had dropped out many moons ago. I did a deal with the owner and swapped him my Volvo saloon for the Bond. After 18 months the car was ready for the road once more; I kept it for 11 years and then sold it to a chap in Fife who later sold it to someone in Co Durham, who, after a year, sold it to a chap on the south coast who immediately put it up for sale at more than double the price he bought it for. I don't know where the car is now but I wish I had kept it. The car won first prize as the best Bond at the National Microcar Rally in 1997."

"I did a deal with the owner and swapped him my Volvo saloon for the Bond. After 18 months the car was ready for the road once more."

David Appleton and his Smart

This Isetta was owned by a member of David's family. The white patch at the top of the open door is due to a repair after the 'bubble' rolled, coming to rest upside down against the kerb; a passer-by had to right the car so the driver could get out.

The Isetta then went to another member of the family who didn't advise the DVLA of change of ownership and left it on a parade ground at Middle Wallop Army Camp; the previous owner had a visit from the police to advise that if it wasn't removed it would be blown-up.

London-based architect David Appleton comes from a long line of microcar owners. "I seemed to grow up surrounded by tales of woe caused by small cars. I think, though, the general consensus was that these traits instilled a personality into the car—car lovers describe this anxiously as 'character'. It must be hereditary as this notion stays with me and the family legends live on. I have lost count of the number of times the 'bubble' was wrapped around various lamp posts by various members of the family, coupled with tales of doors bursting open on sharp corners and brothers, sisters and aunts nearly but not quite falling out of the Mini or, more usually, Midget. And then there was the car that started it all: Grandad's BSA three-wheeler. Was it true that he really yearned for a Kodak camera, but post war these were luxury items so he had to settle for the three-wheeler? The latter had transported my mother as a baby—strapped to the back via some homemade rack due to the lack of seats in the cockpit. I suspect a four-seater wasn't even considered."

"It is difficult to be a car masochist these days and buy something new. The Smart City Coupé seemed to offer some of the old spirit and if the car itself doesn't offer much in terms of unexpected malfunctions then the 'danger seeker' can always venture onto the race track for thrills. The Smart is not really suited to the race track for various reasons, though if the other would-be racers are Smarts too, at least there is a level playing field. Like all cars that live a little on the race track, a disproportionate array of tuning 'mods' are available to lend that elusive 'edge'. Quite how effective these are probably remains confined within the mind of the driver, but they suggest to me the kind of modifications Abarth did to Fiat 500s and Cooper did to Minis in the 1960s. I like to think a little of the ironic energy of the latter cars lives on in mine."

" I have lost count of the number of times the 'bubble' was wrapped around various lamp posts by various members of the family, coupled with tales of doors bursting open on sharp corners and brothers, sisters and aunts nearly but not quite falling out...."

© Mike Baguley.

Steve Denning and his 1954 Fiat Topolino

HRG 348 was Steve's first restoration project. When he acquired the 1954 Fiat Topolino in 1992, it had been off the road for 20 years.

"I'll never forget the look on my wife's face when I brought it home.... I came to see it as a challenge, because so many people had told me the Fiat would never get back on the road."

It took Steve more than 2,000 hours over 26 months to get the car up to 'concours contender'. At its first outing, the car won second place in its class. But for Steve, the reaction of visitors to the Show was as important:

"People would walk past more glamorous cars without a second glance, but they never failed to stop and look at the Topolino."[7]

Since completing this Fiat, Steve has gone on to restore a second car and helped a number of other Topolino owners with their own restoration projects.

Derek and Hazel Cole and their Messerschmitt 'Tiger'

In the mid-1970s, Derek drove his daughter back and forth from school every day in a three-wheeled Messerschmitt—rather than in the family's petrol-hungry Vauxhall Victor estate. He and his wife Hazel kept the Messerschmitt as a second car for a long time. Years later, missing the car, Derek bought another three-wheeler and, eventually, a friend offered him a Messerschmitt Tg500, a 'Tiger', in pieces. He was restoring a Messerschmitt for a friend at the time, so the car stayed in his garage in bits until he had time enough to work on it.

"I'll keep the car until I can't drive it anymore."

John Meadows
and his Frisky

John Meadows is very much part of the 'Frisky Family'. The grandson of Henry Meadows, who founded the company that manufactured the Frisky, John acquired his first Frisky by chance, when he bought a collection of parts from a friend who was emigrating and then had to buy a complete car to see how the pieces would fit together. When John asked what a Frisky was like to drive, his father famously replied: "It's like being dragged along the road with your arse on a shovel." At one point John owned seven Friskys—the full range. Today, he has a Frisky Sport, Coupé and Family Three.

Kevin McCullagh and his Smart

"I work at a product design consultancy in West London and live in East London. I've always lived centrally and avoided cars (for cost and simplicity reasons, rather than having moral objections). I took up the offer of a company car as part of a promotion two years ago, as this took care of much of the cost and hassle. I took delivery of my Smart on the eve of the introduction of the congestion charge... it has cut my commute by 30 minutes."

Jenny and Lawrence House and their collection

Jenny and Lawrence House have been collecting microcars since 1978 when Lawrence was introduced to the cars "by chance", after a schoolfriend had a motorbike accident and was encouraged to replace his bike with a three-wheeler which Lawrence helped to fix. He has continued his restoration projects ever since and, together with his wife Jenny, has assembled a carefully chosen collection of cars and an extensive knowledge of their history.

Otto and Marianne Künnecke, Automuseum Störy

Otto and Marianne Künnecke opened the Automuseum Störy in 1974 having seen the tiny number of microcars in existing auto museums. Of the 140 cars in their collection, their two favourites are a Messerschmitt KR200 and a BMW 600.

"We started in 1972 with 36 cars, not all our own. Marianne and I used to spend weekends visiting auto museums—there were about 30 in Germany then—and we only saw two microcars in all of them.... Cars after 1945 weren't recognised as being collectible then. That's why we decided to open the museum, not just to show them but to get people to drive and restore them."[8]

Steve Hurn
and the buried Isetta

Steve Hurn and his father Mick made the four hour drive from their home in Leicester to a house in Devon to see an Isetta that they had been told about. The house had recently changed hands and, on moving in, the new owner found the Isetta upside down and partially buried in the garden—where it had been for over 20 years. The engine and gearbox had already been removed and, seeing that the car was unsalvageable and knowing that new Isetta parts were already scarce, Steve and Mick decided to recycle the remaining parts to be used to restore other Isettas in a slightly better state.

1959 saw the introduction of the latest member of the Prinz family, the NSU Sport Prinz (the car at the back of this image). With an engine of just under 600cc, the Sport Prinz fulfilled many microcar criteria, while a body designed by Bertone gave it an added style that was aimed at the younger driver.

Rhona and Ken Bell and their Isetta 300

Rhona and Ken Bell initially restored a 1960 Isetta 300 for their daughter. The restoration took two years by which time she had passed her driving test and the Isetta had inspired them to start a collection that now includes a Bond Minicar Mark G Tourer, a 1957 Messerschmitt KR200 and an NSU Sport Prinz.

Andrew Nahum and his Fiat 500

"Although it's fun to drive, and it's really one of the greatest automotive design achievements of all times, for me it's really a machine for parking in. I used to have a piece of concrete at work that no one else could fit into. As the car has such charm, our security guys are great about helping me tuck it in somewhere.

Stef and Bruno Proietti, off London's Caledonian Road, are great at fixing these cars. They can fit disc brakes and all kinds of good things and may make you an espresso—it's like Little Italy up there."

"It's got a 650cc engine from a later Fiat 126 and a few other tweaks that help it stay with the flow of the urban cut and thrust—it's safer not to be too slow."

Mike Shepherd and his Goggomobil, Velorex and Heinkel

"In the early 1970s, I needed a small car to get to work, so I bought a second hand Heinkel. Being a toolmaker, I was able to look after my own cars."

"In about 1958 or 1959, my aunt took me to the seaside in the Isle of Sheppey in her Heinkel. I was about ten. My Mum and my brothers and sisters went on the coach. Then in the early 1970s, I needed a small car to get to work, so I bought a second hand Heinkel. Being a toolmaker, I was able to look after my own cars and I went to the second Burford rally in 1975–owners got together then to swap parts so they could keep the cars on the road. Burford was the catalyst for many of the owners clubs that followed. I was instrumental in starting the Heinkel Owners Club. Now my collection includes a Goggomobil, Velorex, my Heinkel and a Scootacar."

Originally designed as an invalid car and produced under a number of different names, the Velorex was made in Czechoslovakia from 1954. It has a simple construction of fabric stretched over a lightweight frame, though Mike Shepherd's Velorex is made from aluminium panels where fabric was typically used.

Jean Hammond

Jean Hammond runs the Register of Unusual Microcars for microcars of under 700cc, started by Jean and her late husband Edwin. Today there are over 1,000 cars on the register.

"By 1980, we'd got cars scattered around various houses with garages in Sidcup. By this time the garages were costing us a small fortune but you could get three or four of these cars in them. Sidcup was being redeveloped and the big old houses were being pulled down and replaced with small maisonettes and there were all these ladies living in them who didn't use their garages. We used to get people phoning us up from the BBC and ITV to borrow the cars and after that the little old ladies would say 'I've got a car in my garage that's been on television, would you like to see it?' In the end they used to come to us and ask if we had a microcar they could keep in their garage."

David Nancekievill and his 'Primrose'

As a medical student in London, David Nancekievill rode a motorbike and, in the 1960s, bought his first microcar, a Heinkel Trojan, which he drove round the streets of London throughout his studies. Years later, qualified and practising in Harley Street, David revisited his student years and bought 'Primrose', a 1963 Heinkel Trojan that he then painstakingly restored. At the 2004 Classic Cars Live! Show, Primrose won a prize in the Meguiars Concours d'Elegance. 2004 was the first year that microcars took centre stage at the show which featured, in addition to 'Primrose', a Messerschmitt KR200 and a pink 1970 Bond Bug, alongside cars including a 1936 Jensen Ford Shooting Brake, a 1962 Jaguar E-type Roadster and a 1973 Ford Mustang Mach 1.

Jacques Vuillaumier and his Vespa 400

"I bought my first 1957 Vespa 400 in 1961 when I was an engineering student in France after I fell off my Lambretta scooter for the third time. I went on many journeys in the car–during the winter of 1961, my brother Claude and I drove from Paris to Courmayer in Italy for a skiing trip."

"When I left France in 1963 to study in New York at the Columbia Business School, I asked my grandparents to look after my Vespa 400. I drove the car again when I returned to France from New York and I only sold it when I got my first job with 3M France and had enough money to buy a Renault Dauphine. 32 years later, in February 1997, I bought a second 1961 Vespa 400 which I restored. The restoration job was finished in June 2003 just in time for the annual French microcar meeting in Bailleau. I drive my Vespa 400 every weekend to shop in the Paris area."

Ron Arad and his Nissan S-Cargo and Fiat 500

"It's a Nissan S-Cargo, manufactured in 1989, a hybrid between a car, a chariot, a bus and a van. There were only 2,000 of them made by Nissan as a concept car for florists, bakers and so on. I think there are about four or five in England, two of which are mine."

"It looks like someone carried out an exercise in designing a car with just a compass and a ruler, no rogue curves in it. It is tall, you do not have to bend down to get in it, there is plenty of room. Three people can sit in the front, and there is a folding bench in the back. The instruments and the dashboard have a comic-strip simplicity. It is automatic, air-conditioned and the headlamps have silver eyelids."

"Driving it can help you divide people into two distinct categories by their reactions: every traffic light brings an impromptu conference about it."

"It has the genes of the classic Citroën '2' Chevaux, which was my first car, but it is far superior to it, almost like our children are superior to us. It is a pleasure to drive and it makes my poor 1960s Fiat 500 feel sort of jealous and neglected."

Richard Jones
and his Isetta 300

"My Father had an Isetta, and one of my earliest memories is riding in my carrycot on the parcel shelf. Even though my family say that I couldn't possibly remember that, it's a distinct memory to me, coupled with the fact that—though my father had sold the Isetta in 1963—he kept the Cassells book about the Isetta which I used to pore avidly over as a schoolboy."

"I left school and got a job as an apprentice Dental Technician. Being somewhat fitter in those days, I used to cycle the 16 miles from home to work and back and, one day, in 1982, I cycled past an Isetta for sale on the forecourt of a garage. I bought it and kept it for three years, joining the Isetta Owners Club and becoming the club's second Gazette Editor after Tony Marshall. I sold that Isetta and bought an even better one but then I met my future wife, Brenda. Money was tight, and so the car had to go. That didn't stop me wanting another one though and, ten years later, in 1996, I found my present car. My wife went away for three weeks, and I stumbled over the car while she was away."

"When Brenda got back, I told her that our car had broken down on the way to my parents and that it had cost £150 to get fixed. Understandingly, she said, "Oh well, at least you haven't bought an Isetta...."

"It took a year to restore, and since then, my wife and I have been to Germany twice to stay at the Automuseum Störy. I organised the 50th anniversary rally for the Isetta in Brighton, and currently, I organise the Leeds/Bradford microcar clubs summer rally at Snainton, near Pickering."

From left to right: Chris Hopkins, Paul Champney and Richard Jones in 1983 with (left to right); Trojan, Messerschmitt and Isetta © Telegraph & Argus, Bradford.

Gary Hillman
and his Peel Trident

Gary bought this 1966 Peel Trident for his collection of 'extreme and unusual' objects. For Gary, most of the cars he collects express the mood of optimism of the 1950s and 60s when "everyone was trying to invent the transport of the future".

Gary saw a Peel Trident amongst the microcars at the 1997 Christie's auction but decided against bidding for it as he was doing up a house at the time. The Peel sold for far more than its reserve price. Wanting a Trident ever since, Gary tracked this car down and bought it for his collection, as well as a 1965 Amphicar at the same time.

The cars in his collection include a 1959 Cadillac Eldorado Biarritz as well as a Ferrari F512M and he is always on the lookout for new things to add.

Walter Zeichner

Walter Zeichner started his microcar career in an Isetta 250 when he was a student. Money was scarce and the Isetta offered weather protection and a lot of fun for only 200 DM at that time. A growing interest in the history of microcars later led to building up one of the biggest collections of microcar literature worldwide in the 1980s and resulted in a book covering the history of nearly all microcars between 1945 and 1970 worldwide.[9] Some experiences with other small cars followed and his love for under-powered vehicles also led to a considerable collection of motorised bicycles. Today, Walter the author of about 50 books on the history of the motorcar, works for BMW's Mobile Tradition, the heritage centre of the Bavarian Motor Works in Munich. As for microcars, he drives a Messerschmitt KR 200 Cabriolet which he prefers to any other kind of motorised vehicle.

endnotes

1   In the UK, to be eligible for lower
    taxation, three-wheelers could not
    exceed 8cwt (406kg) in weight. This
    limit was revised to 8¼cwt, roughly
    corresponding with the introduction
    of the Reliant 3/25 range.

2   excerpt from *Bubble-cars: a concise
    history*, Herbert, Mark F,
    self-published, 1997.

3   Bobbit, M, *Bubble Cars and
    Microcars*, Marlborough: The
    Crowood Press Ltd, 2003, p. 60.

4   excerpt from Herbert, 1997.

5   *Classic Car Weekly*, 12 March 1997.

6   All prices include 17.5 per cent VAT
    and 15 per cent buyer's premium.

7   The mouse that roared, *Practical
    Classics*, February 1996.

8   *Sports Car International*,
    October/November 1996.

9   Zeichner, W, *Kleinwagen
    International*, Gerlingen:
    Bleicher, 1990.

Chapter Three
Good Things Come In Small Packages

good things come in small packages

In 1958, Cary Grant was wheeled out for the advertising of that year's model of the BMW Isetta 300. The promotional material announced that he was "soon to be seen in *Houseboat*", a film which also featured Sophia Loren. It was a story about the trials and tribulations faced by a father and his three young children in and around a respectable Washington community after the recent death of their mother. Cary Grant's appearance with the Isetta represents one of the earliest versions of what we now readily call 'product placement'. In his mid-fifties in 1958, with films under his belt including *The Philadelphia Story*, *Notorious* and *To Catch a Thief*, Grant's stage persona was a snappily dressed bachelor-about-town, charming and amusing, confident and sophisticated—star qualities it was hoped might rub off on the car. While those in charge of the marketing budget might have recognised the benefits of an association between their car and an A-list star, sadly that relationship had yet to work its magic: the Isetta didn't appear in the actual *Houseboat* movie. Instead Grant drives a 1958 Plymouth, a bright green convertible complete with fins, and an army jeep that comes with his government post (two 1955 Crown Imperial Limousines and a Powerwagon also make an appearance).

Back in Europe the same year, marketing material for the BMW 600 presented the car in a similarly modern, optimistic manner, placing it in front of the Atomium, the futuristic symbol of the 1958 Brussels International Exhibition, with two women planning their visit, sharply dressed in contemporary fashion—the suits, shoes and hairstyles that represented the confident, aspirational spirit of the late 1950s.[1]

Cover of BMW Isetta 300 marketing brochure, 1958.

Right: BMW 600 in front of the Atomium in 1958. The Brussels World's Fair—Expo 58—ran for six months during 1958 and attracted more than 42 million visitors.

©BMW AG Historisches Archiv.

MORE DISTINCTION
MORE VISIBILITY
MORE ROOM
MORE ECONOMY

Isetta 600, circa 1957, set alongside large cars from the luxury end of the market.

It is symptomatic of the way in which microcars were viewed in America at the time that, though marketed as "the most exciting car on the American highway!", the Isetta 300 enjoyed more success in Europe than in the USA—distances were shorter, fuel was more expensive and the tax benefits were greater. Even though it was a remarkably innovative car, this was a time when small cars were even less a part of mainstream American culture than today, but there was another factor. By the end of the 1950s, styling had become embedded as a major driver of consumption and automotive design was not markedly different from its product design cousin as a whole, in that design became a key means for manufacturers to offer choice (and to differentiate their products from those of their rivals), and for consumers to signify their social standing as well as their aspirations for the future. It was almost inevitable that the Isetta would be more successful in Europe than in the USA. Not only was there little incentive to drive a microcar in America, but there was a measure of social and cultural disincentive. With fuel more readily available and distances too long to cover comfortably in a tiny car, any microcar was going to struggle alongside its large car competitors. But the real problem was that no microcar at the time could compete with its larger, streamlined contemporaries in conferring status, something that no amount of association with A-list stars could overcome.

BMW Isetta, circa 1956.

Das spricht für BMW *Isetta*

BMW Isetta, circa 1956.

good things come in small packages   The Macro World of Microcars

In its earliest incarnation, the Isetta was an Italian: the Iso Isetta, developed by engineer Ermenegildo Preti and backed by Milanese businessman and owner of Isotherm Refrigerators, Renzo Rivolta. One of the microcars that spawned the 'bubble car' name because of its most literal 'bubble' shape, the Isetta's form was the result of an endeavour to provide the greatest internal space and maximum strength, but with minimal structure.[2] Neither the complexities of the transition from Iso to BMW, nor the other incarnations of the Isetta, are the tales to tell here[3] but, eventually BMW, needing to find a catalyst to reinvigorate post war business, acquired the Iso design and went into manufacture in Germany in 1955 with the BMW Isetta. A larger version, the BMW 600, followed in 1957 but never quite addressed what was required in a larger car and was less successful in commercial terms.

A glance back at the early formation of the automobile is needed here. Today, the motorcar is a century old and it is possible to trace its formal conventions back to the origins of pre-motorised transport. In *A Century of Car Design*, Penny Sparke explains how the mould was set for what became the established form for the automobile:

> Like so many of the other goods that made up the visual landscape of the twentieth century, in terms of its social and cultural functions it [the car] retained one foot in the past for some time. The carriage lent it its early format and it took a few decades for it to break loose from the powerful precursor and, aesthetically, throw off its heritage.[4]

Sparke maps the evolution of car design and shows how the development of the unitary car (built as a single structure rather than a combination of chassis and body) gave the automobile a more coherent look while leading to further changes to its appearance:

> A sequence of developments—among them the raising of the bonnet and the lowering of the sitting position of the rear passengers—meant that the car acquired a strong horizontal emphasis and a 'waistline' that held the components together visually.[5]

Whilst the amount of conscious design input into microcars varies and is, in some cases, more or less non-existent, formal developments can nonetheless be perceived throughout generations of microcars. Some were based more on engineering than design principles and although there are stylish as well as cheap microcars, all share a focus on economy over appearance. It is no coincidence that the car often seen as setting an early benchmark for the microcar—the Topolino—was developed by Dante Giacosa, an engineer able to integrate principles of both design and engineering.

Although there are stylish as well as cheap microcars, all share a focus on economy over appearance.

In the beginning the basis for mainstream automotive production was utility. Cars such as Henry Ford's Model T which brought the possibility of transport to thousands, epitomised this principle. However, throughout the twentieth century, this was gradually usurped by an emphasis on design.

> To Ford, the car was an absolute democratic necessity, a utilitarian tool, an expression of man's ingenuity and his freedom. To Alfred Sloan, the founder of General Motors, that same car represented an opportunity to seduce the consumer with ideas of social competition and cultural modelling which are still with us today.... It was Sloan who had no less an idea... that consumers might be persuaded to buy more cars, more expensively, more often if those cars were styled....[6]

Efforts to reflect changes in customer taste and to drive sales generated the establishment of departments within the major motor companies dedicated to styling. This development subsequently led to the 'annual model change', through which manufacturers sought to sustain sales by ensuring consumer need for 'this year's model'. Promotional exhibitions such as 'Motoramas', first held in the United States in the early 1950s, introduced the idea of testing, or even subtly dictating, public opinion by showing 'dream cars', concept cars that may never go into production but were sufficiently futuristic in design to be a clear gauge of the boundaries beyond which the public would not venture as consumers.

The annual model changes established in the mainstream automotive industry became a key part of the microcar sector too, leading to developments and improvements to individual marques year on year. In Great Britain, each model of the Bond Minicar, produced in Marks A to G over a decade and a half, introduced some significant incremental improvements on the previous year's model. Meanwhile, in the United States, later models of the Crosley, bowing to pressure from dealers and customers, offered options for both interior upholstery and exterior colour.

In post war America, the evolution of the car into a status symbol, "an emblem of conspicuous consumption in itself"[7], as much as if not more than a means of transport, made it difficult for the small car, let alone the microcar, to gain a foothold in the mainstream automotive market. Vast distances coupled with cheap petrol and negligible car taxes made for an inhospitable environment for small cars in general.

> As Americans moved into cities and became mobile as never before, a useful car was no longer enough. They wanted to be able to outdo their neighbours and use their cars as a means of expressing their fashionable lifestyles.... Henry Ford had had the vision to realize that the potential for car ownership was enormous, and in the early century ownership of a Model T Ford had been, in itself, enough to confer a high level of status on these new customers. Harley Earl went one stage further. He realized that, once car ownership was more or less universal, Americans would want more from these feats of modern technology than mere reliability and low price. He went on to transform the automobile from an engineered object to a stylish consumer artifact....[8]

"As Americans moved into cities and became mobile as never before, a useful car was no longer enough. They wanted to be able to outdo their neighbours and use their cars as a means of expressing their fashionable lifestyles...."
Penny Sparke

Pre war Crosley convertible sedan and delivery vehicle.

Although a number of surveys of the American car-buying public indicated that there was interest in the small car, "few automakers believed Americans would make any trade in appearance, performance and ride for lower cost. And there was still another factor: money. "The Big Three"[9] had sunk more than $25 million into assembly lines, and converting to small car production would require millions more. It was a frightening gamble on an uncertain product."[10]

Before the Second World War, Powel Crosley, an American refrigerator magnate, developed a small car specifically intended to be low in cost and maintenance. His approach to manufacturing echoed Ford's; he believed that those people who made his products should be able to afford them. Sales of Crosley cars, both before and after the war, were good but, even so, production ceased in 1952.

> Though the Crosley could be considered cute, it did nothing to enhance an individual's social status. But, unless you were there, it is hard to visualize that there was a time, as in the post World War Two days, when cars were in desperately short supply. Buyers had the money, but there was little to buy. The Crosley was better than nothing and it was, after all, transportation. Crosley never looked at his post war success as a positive result of the supply-and-demand law however, but as support for his idea of what the US family car ought to be.[11]

"Unless you were there, it is hard to visualize that there was a time, as in the post World War Two days, when cars were in desperately short supply. Buyers had the money, but there was little to buy."
Vince Agul

necessity is the mother of invention

The microcar was the antithesis of the luxury car, but inevitably borrowed styling cues from that end of the spectrum. Many of the cues were pared down, for example, running boards were often reduced or removed entirely to save material and weight and to maximise interior space while minimising external dimensions. The range of microcar design has always been wide, with some taking their cues from mainstream vehicle design, while others, combining motorcycle and automotive design and engineering approaches, reverted to an earlier aesthetic. Many microcars went against the grain of mainstream automotive design, being low-tech solutions to transport needs, although the transfer of technology from, for example, the aircraft industry into microcar development was important.

The post war lack of materials was common to all nations: shortages of wide sheet steel were particularly problematic to the automotive industry. In the UK, financing new ventures was difficult so, rather than develop new ideas, the industry reinstated pre war designs. Ironically, Germany, with most of its plants destroyed and Marshall Aid coming in, had a much better start and began designing from scratch. In some cases, existing automotive manufacturers were continuing production interrupted by the Second World War. In others, manufacturers previously unknown for car manufacture were diversifying into new sectors in order to survive the post war period. As a result, some of the cars were clearly an evolution of pre war styling, based on models of car design introduced during the early stages of the automotive industry. Other manufacturers threw away the rule book and, as far as was possible within established practices in car design and existing manufacturing processes, started anew, re-defining and developing the design of the small car. Cars needed to be cheap to buy and to run. Across Europe and the United States, people were desperate to get going and manufacturers—looking for a means of economic survival—were only too pleased to plug that particular gap in the market.

Some of the cars were clearly an evolution of pre war styling, based on models of car design introduced during the early stages of the automotive industry. Other manufacturers threw away the rule book and, as far as was possible within established practices in car design and existing manufacturing processes, started anew....

Some ingenious solutions were conceived to solve the problems that came with producing lightweight, economical vehicle. The first Topolino's 'packaging' (the overall way in which a car is put together), achieved maximum internal space for the size of the car through a novel arrangement of the required set of component parts—maximising the interior width by bowing the body sides and introducing sliding windows in order to eliminate the need for double-lined door panels. The design and arrangement of windows—what car designers call DLO or 'daylight opening'— is important in automotive design in general and the range of solutions to providing windows that are both mechanically simple and cheap is striking in the microcar. The main mechanisms included sliding, hinged, pivoting and winding versions (sliding windows made hand signals awkward—and therefore potentially less clear and effective—but winding windows were expensive).

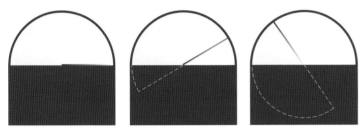

The windows in the Champion 400 (a German microcar of the early 1950s) were wound around a central axis so that they were 'stored' in the door lining when the window was open.

The Bond Minicar[12] was known for its ability to turn its front wheel by 180 degrees lock-to-lock so that it could turn in an extremely tight radius, while many microcars were able to change the direction of the running of the engine in order to engage either forward or reverse gear. This meant, at the furthest extreme, that some microcars had four forward and four reverse gears.

Detail of Lloyd Alexander brochure showing pivoting windows, 1958.

BMW Isetta, 1957—see the cleaner lines achieved by the sliding, rather than pivoting, windows.

necessity is the mother of invention

The Macro World of Microcars

In late 1952, *Autocar* rounded up new developments in the small car market, reporting that a small number of manufacturers were developing—with difficulty—a new type of "smaller, simpler and cheaper" economy car for the European market: "Something new, something cheaper to buy and to operate, is [therefore] required, and it cannot be obtained by scaling down existing models. Designers and sales staff are deeply engaged at present in deciding what must be sacrificed; for an entirely new approach is essential."[13]

Many existing mechanical components—from the motorcycle industry, for example—were transferred to the manufacture of microcars. However borrowing existing car components remained more difficult:

> It is worth mentioning some of the difficulties that beset the designers of a car of this type. It is important that such a vehicle should feel like a 'real car', and perform at least well enough to keep up with the speed of an average traffic stream; yet if it is to be really economical it must have a small engine and be of light weight. A high initial price tends to defeat the object of the car, and small firms who have entered this field have been faced with the problem of not being able to use many components common to cars produced in large numbers. Door handles, for example, in the range available from component manufacturers are too big and heavy, but to have them made specially makes the car expensive. Consequently, entry into the economy field by a firm with resources for high output—and thus reduced cost—is welcome.[14]

"It is important that such a vehicle should feel like a 'real car', and perform at least well enough to keep up with the speed of an average traffic stream; yet if it is to be really economical it must have a small engine and be of light weight."
Autocar

Details from a Nobel 200 brochure, circa 1957.

entrepreneurs and designers

The individualistic nature of the microcar world extends to those responsible for their design and production. From Giovanni Michelotti and Dante Giacosa, Powel Crosley and Lawrence Bond to Egon Brütsch and David Gottlieb, a number of key people were involved in the development of the microcar. They came from conventional automotive design, from engineering, from motor racing and from business. Two common characteristics prevail: a degree of entrepreneurship and a desire to push boundaries.

Designers and manufacturers were featured prominently in the press and even appeared in the marketing material for the cars. In fact, autobiographies of the people involved in the making of the cars still retain a unique fascination and remain significant to the ways in which these cars are seen by contemporary owners and collectors. However, their jobs were sometimes far from secure. With production numbers ranging from a single car, often a prototype that never made it into production, to hundreds of thousands of a single make or model, the development of microcars often resembled a lottery rather than an industry. Not surprisingly, the practice of a single engineer or designer working on an idea for a small car in the hope that it might some day go into production was a common phenomenon in the world of the microcar.

They also shared a gender: while a number of women are associated with different marques, most often in the context of marketing, as in the more mainstream automotive design context, none is central to microcar design or manufacture.

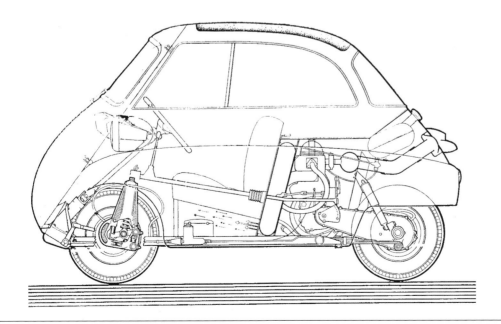

marketing and press

The motoring press were, in the main, full of—measured—praise for the new cars as they came on the market, seeing them as meeting a highly pressing need. There were dissenters but it would have been harsh, indeed inappropriate, to criticise these contributions to post war recovery. Descriptions like "fascination and admiration", "straightforward, simple design", "unique little car" and "ingenious and practical features" prevailed.

Many of the three-wheelers were reviewed in the motorcycle as well as automotive press, inevitably resulting in the evaluation being by comparison to two-wheeled transport. Here, microcars managed to maintain their status. The AC Petite Mark 2, for example, was described as:

> Smooth, comfortable, economical—yet capable of taking Mr and Mrs Everyman, plus one child, plus luggage, anywhere they wish at a speed more than adequate for touring... that's the Petite Mark 2. Its predecessor has already earned a special place in utility motoring—nothing seems more certain that this 1956 version will consolidate it.[15]

And the Heinkel was praised as: "A German cabin-scooter offering motorcycle economy with small car accommodation. A performance which astonished the tester, and which delighted the laymen (and women) carried as passengers."[16]

In performance terms, the industry stressed the relationship between these tiny cars and their more conventional relations[17]:

> Good performance is essential; you do not want thousands of underpowered miniatures obstructing other vehicles. The economy car must have every component designed and stressed for this particular job....[18]

"Good performance is essential; you do not want thousands of underpowered miniatures obstructing other vehicles."
Autocar

BMW Isetta, circa 1958.

Goggomobil, 1957.

Overall, apart from on the 'cool' rating, the microcar came out ahead of the motorcycle. The marketing of many of the cars, whilst not necessarily making explicit the comparison between car and bike, majored on purchase and running cost, fuel economy, durability and maintenance, safety and protection from the weather. With some notable exceptions, the notion of styling, chic or cool remained low on the list of noteworthy characteristics.

Microcars were marketed at different times and in different countries through a combination of finance and fashion, economy and style. But from the second half of the 1950s, the era of the Atomium and the Isetta, the somewhat austere models of the immediate post war period had made room for more confident and flamboyant microcars. The marketing of cars as economic to buy and run was joined by advertising that was stylish, forward-looking and aspirational.

Heinkel, circa 1956.

BMW Isetta, 1959.

Reliant Regal, mid-1950s.

Fiat 500, 1967.

BMW Isetta, circa 1957/1958.

The Cars

Many **microcars**, particularly those mass produced to any extent, underwent a succession of changes ranging from the minute—known to those who know the cars best—to the more substantial modifications that were advertised to the buying public. Many of the **microcars** shown here are part of a **'family' of cars** in which each is as important as any other. They are chosen as representatives of their marques and are intended to be a way into understanding these vehicles, not through exhaustive descriptions, but original contexts and imaginative visuals.

AC Petite

UK 1953-1958

Made a Little Better than it Need Be.

The AC Petite (Mark 1 in 1953 followed by Mark 2 in 1955) was made by the British company AC Cars Ltd. Known for "placing the accent on comfort rather than sheer economy", the first Petite had a 353cc engine and sold for just over £300/$510.

"A vehicle conceived for the genteel and sedate market formed by those whose preference is for a small four-wheeler, but whose pockets are not deep enough to shoulder the heavy running costs which even small car ownership entails."[19]

"Wives find it so simple to drive for shopping or taking the children to school, when the husband isn't using it to cut costs in travelling to work."

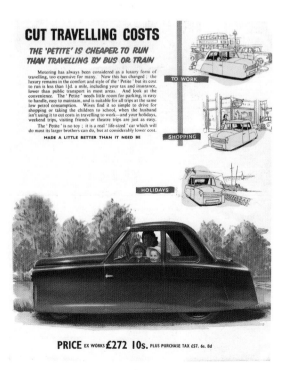

AC Petite, mid-1950s.

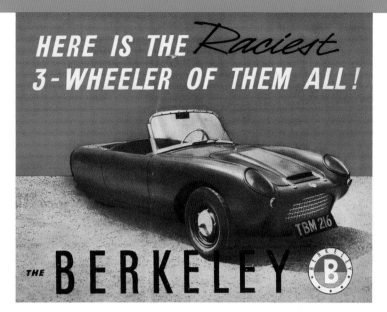

Berkeley, circa 1959.

Berkeley
UK 1956-1959

The BERKELEY for glamour, performance and economy.

Responsible for the Bond Minicar, Lawrence (Lawrie) Bond also designed the Berkeley, developing the first prototypes in 1956– "a new approach to the problem of how to build a car".[20] Initially a caravan manufacturer, Berkeley developed the use of fibreglass for the shells of its touring caravans, transferring this expertise and skill with fibreglass to Berkeley cars. The Berkeley was manufactured in three sections of moulded fibreglass. And with any of the sections suffering damage they could be replaced independently of the others. The Berkeley was introduced as a sports car, with "sports car zip": *Autocar*'s 1957 road test of the two-seater suggested that "this car really does have sporting characteristics, while also being a satisfactory means of economy transport... a delightful miniature sports car".[21]

The range of models across the four years of production included two- and four-seaters and three- and four-wheeled versions with engine sizes from 322 to 692cc. Prices ranged between £400/$680 and £700/$1,190.

BERKELEY

foursome

Here for the first time is a car which gives you sports car zip and performance plus really good carrying capacity.

A true 4-seater, the Berkeley Foursome has ample room in the back seats for two. Alternatively you will find you can fit in a surprising amount of luggage, golf clubs or other gear.

Developed from the 492 c.c. 2-seater, whose reliability has been proved in scores of rallies, the Berkeley Foursome enables you to go places fast—*and* take more with you.

BERKELEY CARS LTD., BIGGLESWADE, BEDS, ENGLAND

Berkeley Foursome, circa 1958.

BMW Isetta
Germany/UK 1955-1964
Isetta 600 Germany 1957-1959

First produced with a 250cc engine, the Isetta was sold overseas to countries including the United States, generally with a 295cc engine, as well as some modified styling. Marketing for the car stressed all the usual positive microcar attributes such as "motor-cycle economy with all the comfort and safety of a car". However, by photographing the Isetta with a range of contemporary stars (including Elvis Presley) and emphasising the car's 'fun' factor, the Isetta attained an extra dimension which—coupled with its highly recognisable styling—lent the car a character over and above one of utility transport. The Isetta's unique quality is principally achieved through its innovative design which had, right from the start, sought to develop a *small* car rather than a scaled-down version of a conventionally sized one. Not surprisingly, the Isetta has always been known far beyond the cognoscenti, and continues to be one of the most enduring icons of the microcar world. Around 160,000 Isettas were made in Germany, with the car also being manufactured in Britain.

"The Isetta is unusual in a number of ways. Not the least of these is its place mid-way between full-sized car and motorcycle, with considerable appeal to owners of both. Sporting enough in performance to relieve the monotony for a motorcyclist seeking better weather protection, it is sufficiently refined for the motorist compelled to look for extreme economy."[22]

The Isetta underwent a series of small alterations to its design, with BMW also offering a version with a cargo platform. In 1956, the Isetta's window design was modified; a cleaner line was achieved by replacing the swivelling 'quarter lights' with sliding windows (BMW referred to the first 'bubble window' as "Standard", while the sliding version was "Export").

We went one better—and bought an Isetta.

"So many economy cars call for manipulation of some comic feature, either a special type of gear-change, an unusual method of starting, very odd steering or a lack of brakes. The Isetta suffers from none of these and everything is worked by normal car practice, even the starter being brought into play by merely turning the ignition key".[23]

In 1957, BMW launched the 600, a different vehicle but with comparable styling and the same recognisable front-opening door as the 300. "Extremely neat detail design is evident, the decorative slats on the rear quarter panels being in fact air intake louvers for the rear engine."[24]

Isetta 600, circa 1957.

Isetta 600, circa 1957.

The Cars   The Macro World of Microcars

BMW Isetta magazine advertisment in *The Motor*, April 1957.

BMW Isetta, circa 1956.

Bond Bug

UK 1970-1974

Bond Bug, circa 1970.

"The man we're after is one who's full of sport, fun and energy who wants a vehicle purely for fun purposes and fun transport. That's what we were after in the first place. Then, as the car started to develop we began to feel that what we had got was not just a replacement for the old motorcycle but a new fun motor car. The fact that it has three wheels is quite incidental. It's a new form of transport."[25]

At its launch in 1970, three versions of the Bond Bug were offered, all in the characteristic 'tangerine': the basic Bug 700 (around £548/$932), the 700E (around £579/$984) and the 700ES (around £629/$1,069). Only one 700 was produced. The Bond Bug, with its unique and radical new styling by Ogle Design, was aimed at a younger, trend-conscious market. In order to attract younger buyers its purchase was made as simple, economical and attractive as possible by offering a package that included two years road tax, a preferential insurance rate and an extended warranty. After over 2,000 sales, production ceased in 1974.

"The steering is real Graham Hill stuff. A tiny simulated leather rim steering wheel is ideal for a straight arm driving position... and only requires just over half a turn to hold the front wheel on a 15 metres diameter circle. So driving in town the position of the hands on the wheel never changes...."[26]

Bond Minicar Mark A-G
UK 1949-1966

Lawrence (Lawrie) Bond, British motor racing enthusiast and designer of the Berkeley, was also responsible for the Bond Minicar, one of the most popular British microcars. The Minicar evolved from the Mark A in 1949 to the Mark G which ended production in 1966, with more sophisticated modifications and increased engine sizes being applied year on year. The first model, the Mark A, with a 122cc engine, was without doors or a reverse gear, and sold for just under £200/$340. The Mark C, at 197cc, was available with modifications, including an electrical ignition system. By the Mark E, the car offered doors, indicators and more. Marks F and G had a larger engine size of 246cc and an increase in weight to match, a hard top and wind-up windows. The styling of the Mark C gave the car an appearance very distinct from previous models. The front grille was modified and front wings, incorporating the headlights, were introduced either side, giving the car a far more coherent appearance. Although design modifications continued, this established the general form for subsequent models. One of the best known attributes of the Bond Minicar, from the Mark C onwards, is the ability to turn the complete front wheel unit 180 degrees.

Early 1950s Minivan and Minitruck manufactured by Sharp's Commercials Ltd.

Autocar, reviewing the Mark C on its debut, stressed the sensible, utilitarian characteristics of the car:

"Although only a three-wheeler, the Bond Mark C is a two- or four-seater that can claim to be a useful means of transport likely to appeal as a second car, or to those who do not have to travel far afield in the course of their day-to-day affairs…. It is known that some of these cars have completed long Continental trips. This confirms that the Bond is capable of long journeys. Such work is not its forte, however, but it does provide economical transport for local use."[27]

But by Mark F, *Motor Cycling* said: "Since its inception towards the end of the 40s, the Bond 'Minicar' in all of its continually improved versions, has built up a formidable reputation as an economy vehicle offering complete enclosure on three wheels at well below conventional car first-price and running costs. Moreover, it has become renowned for possessing manoeuvrability par excellence—a facet of considerable importance in narrow country lanes and also in the congested city streets of the post war era."[28]

Bond Minicar Mark C, 1956.

Crosley
USA 1939-1942/1946-1952

Powel Crosley produced small, economical cars before and after the Second World War. His principal concern was to keep the purchase price and running costs low. In order to do this, the early cars that rolled off the assembly lines were basic in specification, with no interior trim and a painted 'serviceable gray'.[29] During wartime fuel rationing, Crosleys, which had attracted reasonable sales in the United States before the war, were being bought on the used car market for their fuel efficiency at prices three or four times their original selling price.

Why buy a battleship to cross a river when a rowboat will get you there just as well?[30]

A publicity-savvy entrepreneur, Crosley was already known for the development and manufacturer of refrigerators and a low-cost radio set that sold for $19.95/£12 in a 1940s market in which radios could cost more than $100/£59.

Pre and post war, Crosley cars sold in the thousands, but eventually production ceased in 1952: "We couldn't make the car at a low enough price to attract enough buyers because of rising costs. The only way a small car can compete with a conventional-size car is by having a particularly attractive selling price."[31]

"There is no machine so perfect that it can be improved by discarding some too expensive or complicated part, and substituting an equally efficient short cut."[32]
Powel Crosley

Pre war Crosley convertible coupe.

Fiat Topolino 500A (Little Mouse)

Italy 1936-1955 (as Fiat 500 A, B and C)

Topolino 500A, 1936 © Fiat.

"Its diminutive size and striking body lines aroused interest wherever our journeying took us over our weekend test.... A baby it may be, but it is a lively youngster and an excellent companion on the open road...."[33]

Launched at the Milan Motor Show in 1936 and introduced to the UK at the Olympia show in the same year, the first Topolino, was designed to provide comfortable and economical motoring for two adults (plus luggage, or two small children[sic]). The convertible saloon version, with a 570cc engine, sold for £120/$204 in 1937.

"Freedom of movement for elbows and plenty of clearance for hats..."[34]

There was general agreement across the UK motoring press that the first Fiat 500 had set the design standards for the smaller car with much of its success coming from the fact that Dante Giacosa developed both the car's engineering and its styling.

"Frankly we are surprised—surprised that so small a car as the Fiat '500' can give the illusion of being a much bigger model... and that it can perform so brightly when it is realised that it only has a 570cc engine."[35]

The car offered "only two seats and two doors, but was smaller and cheaper to operate than any of its competitors. It opened up an entirely new market, whose existence had not hitherto been recognised, and many people who already owned a car could not resist buying it as a runabout."[36]

The following year several manufacturers were rumoured to be experimenting with 'baby' cars and the Topolino and the generations of Fiat 500s that were to follow became a benchmark for small car design.

Fiat 600
Italy 1955-1960

Initially the replacement for the Topolino in 1955, the 600 range was eventually to include three versions: the standard saloon, convertible (with 'sunshine' roof) and the 4/5 or 6 person Multipla.[37]

"... the Fiat 600 is one of those original designs which creates another milestone in the history of motoring.... The 600 does not give the impression of a big car scaled down, and the performance on the road is impressive when the engine size is kept in mind."[38]
Autocar

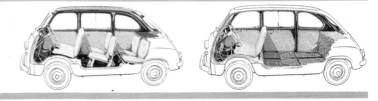

Fiat 600D, late 1950s.

Fiat 600, circa 1956.

The Cars   The Macro World of Microcars

Fiat Nuova 500
Italy 1957-1960

Forever to be associated with Italian style and chic, the Fiat Nuova 500 was recently placed seventh in *Car* magazine's "top 100 coolest cars".[39] Since the launch of the Topolino in 1936, the 500 has seen seven main versions—from the 500A, to the Fiat Nuova of 1957, to its last incarnation, the 500R—and has formed the basis of a number of other small cars. This diversity has made the Fiat 500 series one of the best-loved and most influential car families to date.

"The conception and design has been brilliantly balanced between the need to provide a real miniature car without unorthodoxy, and to permit economical production."[40]
Autocar

The arrival of the 1957 Nuova 500 marked a truly significant moment for the Fiat family; with its 479cc engine and its sharp styling, it was destined to become hugely popular.

Changes to the 500 have included the replacement of the 'suicide' doors (rear-hinged) with front-hinged doors, increased safety features, larger windscreen area and higher performance.

"It is a sound engineering job into the bargain."[41]

mot, August 1960.

Fiat 500, circa 1967.

Fiat 500, circa 1967.

Fiat 500, circa 1967.

The Cars   The Macro World of Microcars

Fiat Stationwagon
Italy 1960-1977

The 1960 Fiat Stationwagon, the 'Giardiniera' was a version of the 500 developed to carry up to four passengers plus luggage or driver alone with a load of up to 250kg.

"The Italians match their affinity with micro-motoring to a happy flair for making little cars really well, and within the limitations of its body dimensions and engine power, the Giardiniera is a minor masterpiece."[42]

Fiat 500 stationwagon, mid-1960s.

Frisky

UK 1957-1964

Known for its Michelotti (the father of the first Ferrari) styling, the Frisky was initially seen as a prototype—with four wheels and gullwing doors—at the Geneva Motor Show in March 1957. After this first appearance, the car underwent some modifications in design and construction. After its showing at London's Earl's Court Motor Show later the same year, the car was manufactured as the Frisky Sport, with four wheels, soft top and chic styling. A four-wheeled, hard top version of the Sport followed—the Frisky Coupé which *Autocar* described as appealing because of its "appearance, performance and economy".[43]

In 1958, again at the Earl's Court Motor Show, two new Friskys were unveiled. One, the Frisky Sprint, pushed the boundaries of small car design further, but was never to be produced in the UK.[44] The other car to be launched at the Show was the most successful Frisky—the Family Three. On the market in 1959, this hard top Frisky, with its lower price and three-wheel tax benefits, was destined to become the range's best seller.

Frisky Family Three Four Seater

★ *ELEGANT*
★ *ECONOMICAL*
★ *ROOMY*
★ *RELIABLE*

Styled by the famous Italian designer GIOVANNI MICHELOTTI

Frisky Family Three, circa 1959.

Frisky

Sports and Coupe

The modern car for Personal Transport

styled by the famous Italian designer **GIOVANNI MICHELOTTI**

Frisky Sport, 1959.

Glas Goggomobil T250-TS400
Germany 1955-1969

Go buy Goggo: the wonder baby car.

Glas, the manufacturer of the Goggomobil range, which included a series of small cars and vans, was one of the most successful of the microcar manufacturers. Glas had moved into automotive manufacture–via scooters–from the production of agricultural equipment.

Well received by the German public from its introduction in the mid-50s, the first Goggomobil, the T250, was a four-wheeler with a 247cc engine. Its success led to the car being given a larger 293cc engine and renamed the T300–this model was exported to the UK as the Regent in 1956. At around £500/$850, the Goggomobil was expensive as an import, but the car was welcomed by the automotive press as a valuable addition to the post war small car market.

Autosport described the Goggomobil as "a real little motor car in its own right".[45] 10 inch wheels were used; allowing for maximum interior space (larger wheels would intrude into the driver and passenger space, particularly when turning). The diminutive wheel size contributed to the car's appearance as a scaled down family car. It had a strangely conventional shape that, nonetheless, remains distinctive amongst the range of microcars.

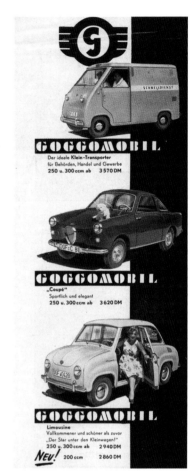

Goggomobil range, 1956.

"For those who wish to buy a small car with safety as well as economy, excellent manoeuvrability, and a certain character, a Goggo would make a first-class buy."[46]

THE NEW POPULAR CAR FOR FAMILY MOTORING

Goggomobil, 1956.

THE LATEST MODEL — A FULL 4-SEATER WITH THE NEW 400 cc ENGINE

Space for four adults · excellent suspension · rapid acceleration · high speed · excellent roadholding · low maintenance costs · robust chassis · easy manoeuvrability.
A demonstration run in this car will convince you more readily than a long description by us.

Goggomobil, circa1958.

Heinkel
Germany 1956-1959

Heinkel, circa 1956.

Trojan 200, circa 1963.

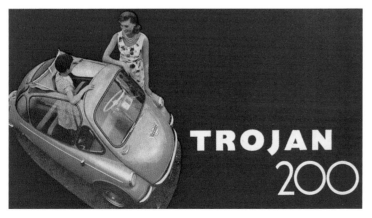

Trojan 200, circa 1963.

"Economy of fuel such as it would be hard to better in any other vehicle with side-by-side seating makes the Heinkel Cabin Cruiser extremely interesting to British motorists at the present time. It has, however, a more enduring interest, as being about the lightest and smallest-engined vehicle offering standards of comfort, refinement and performance acceptable to owners of orthodox modern cars".[47]

Known for aircraft design and manufacture, Ernst Heinkel needed to diversify post war, and moved into automobile production. The first commercially produced vehicle from Heinkel was the 150cc Tourist scooter first seen in 1953.

Looking to improve on the Iso Isetta, Ernst Heinkel developed the first Heinkel microcar and, after a delay agreed with BMW to allow the launch of the BMW Isetta, the Heinkel 150 (three wheels and a 174cc engine) appeared on the market in 1956. Models with increased engine sizes and three and four wheels followed. While there appear to be similarities between the Isetta and the Heinkel, on closer examination, the two cars have identifiable differences, including the Heinkel's slightly elongated shape, giving it more internal space.

For a short period of particularly high sales, Heinkels were transported by plane, five at a time, from Hanover in Germany to Croydon in the UK.

Trojan 200
UK 1962-1965

From 1958, production of the Heinkel began under license in Ireland, as the Heinkel-I. In 1962, the Irish company producing the Heinkel-I sold the rights to Trojan, a company based in Croydon and production of the Trojan began. Two models were produced—four- wheeled and three-wheeled—the latter being the Trojan 200. However, sales began to decline in the mid-1960s and production finally ceased in 1965.

"Climb inside this particular bubble and you'll be amazed at the amount of space."[48]

Lloyd Alexander
Germany 1958-1961

The first German Lloyd microcar, the 300, was produced from 1950.[49] Looking back at the development of the Lloyd in 1957, motoring journalist Gordon Wilkins described the first Lloyd as "a crude little contraption with two-stroke engine, front wheel drive, an unlovely body in wood and fabric and springing that was like sliding down stairs on a tea-tray, but it held together and cost little to run".[50]

Lloyd cars were improved model by model until, in 1958, the Alexander was produced, closely followed by its cousin the TS (Touring Sport) a four-wheeled, four-seater with luggage space and "equipment which would be regarded as de luxe on many larger cars—self-parking wipers, a screen-washer, asymmetrical half-beam lamps, twin sun visors, armrests to the rear bench, clothes peg, a parking lamp, two ashtrays and headlamp flashing switch."[51]

By 1958, Lloyds were being manufactured at a rate of 52,000[52] each year and were in production until 1962, by which time over 300,000 cars had been made.

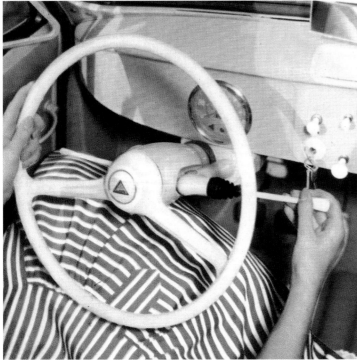

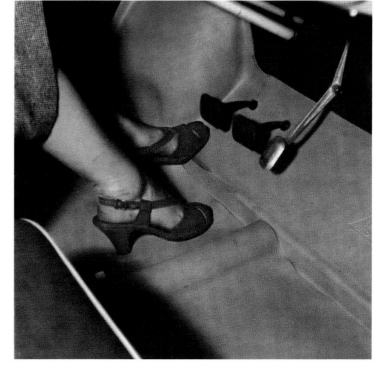

Lloyd Alexander, 1958.

Messerschmitt KR200 and Tg500
Germany 1953-1964

Based on designs for an invalid carriage developed by German engineer Fritz Fend, and taken to production by former aircraft manufacturer Messerschmitt, the first Messerschmitt microcar, the KR175, was launched at the Geneva Motor Show in 1953. With its remarkable appearance—a three-wheeler steered by handlebars, with the passenger sitting behind the driver, protected by a domed canopy hinged along one side—the car attracted immediate attention, both positive and negative.

Manufactured until the mid-1950s, the KR175 reached production figures of nearly 20,000 and was to be followed, in early 1955, by a more powerful and refined version, the KR200; export models were produced for countries including Spain and the UK.

A transfer of production in 1957 from Messerschmitt to Fahrzeug und Maschinenbau Regensburg GmbH saw a change of logo to the three linked diamonds and initials seen on post-1957 models.

With one or two other variations on the way, the Messerschmitt was taken to new heights with the development of the Tg500, introduced in 1957. Known as the 'Tiger', this model was based on the KR200 but had four wheels and a larger engine, accompanied by more modified styling but with increased performance. Fewer than 1,000 'Tigers' were made and those that have survived are highly cherished.

The ,**Messerschmitt**' Sports Saloon as a result of development over a long period is a most reliable vehicle which can be maintained and serviced by anyone without technical knowledge.

The ,**Messerschmitt**' Sports Cabrio complete with heater is the latest addition to the ,Messerschmitt' range.
ALL MODELS AVAILABLE IN MANY ATTRACTIVE COLOURS.

Messerschmitt Tg500, 1958.

Messerschmitt KR200, late 1950s.

Messerschmitt KR200 De Luxe, late 1950s.

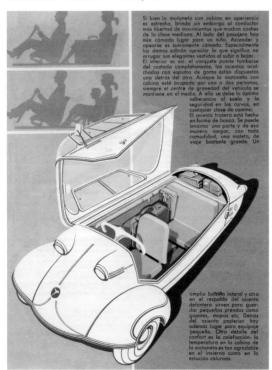

Spanish version of Messerschmitt KR200, late 1950s.

Messerschmitt KR200 De Luxe, late 1950s.

Nobel 200 and Nobel Sporty in front of the Atomium.

Nobel 200
UK 1959-1962

The Nobel was based on the German Fuldamobil, a microcar
that was very popular in its home country. Fuldamobil sold licenses
across the world which resulted in Fuldamobils being produced in
countries including Norway, Greece, Chile, Zimbabwe and the UK.[53]
The S7 range was introduced in Germany in 1957, and the Nobel
200 was a version of the Fuldamobil S7 built under license.
The 200 was made and assembled by a number of different
manufacturing concerns—initially, the chassis came from
Birmingham, fibreglass bodies from Bristol and engines
from Germany, with all being assembled in Northern Ireland.

Remember, those low sleek lines are achieved without sacrificing space or comfort... and there is performance to match this modern appearance—swift acceleration—effortless fast cruising!

THE **NOBEL 200**........

TRAVEL IN STYLE FOR HALF A PENNY A MILE

YN 200

Nobel 200, circa 1957.

Nobel 200, circa 1958.

L'Oeuf
France 1942

French industrial designer Paul Arzens—better known for his train designs—built this city car in Paris in 1942. Polished aluminium and plexiglass (at the time only recently introduced in France), the L'Oeuf was powered by an electric motor, and had a range of 150kmh and a top speed of 75kmh. The car never went into production but is still exhibited today in the Musée de Mulhouse in the south of France.[54]

L'Ouef, 1942 © Roger-Viollet/Rex Features.

Opperman Unicar
UK 1956-1959

Opperman Unicar, circa 1958.

At just under £400/$680, the Unicar was the cheapest car on offer at the 1956 London Motor Show. A *Top Gear* road test described the Unicar as "one of the most interesting miniature motor cars outside the three-wheeler class manufactured in Britain today".

"We appreciate that manufacturers of this type of car are in a difficult position, of course. The natural tendency is to cut the price of the car to the lowest possible and it has to be admitted that when a machine is built down to a price the results are often unsatisfactory. Many drivers are showing considerable interest in these small four-wheeled cars and it can be said that where first cost is of extreme importance the Unicar has much to offer."[55]

Opperman Stirling
UK 1958-1959

Announced at the Earl's Court Motor Show in 1958, *The Motor* described the follow up to the Unicar, the Stirling, as "…a new, larger and more handsome model which for its looks alone could be labelled a miniature Grand Tourer."[56] Unfortunately only two prototypes were ever made.

Opperman Stirling, 1958.

ALMOST CHEAPER
THAN
WALKING!

Peel P50, mid-1960s.

Peel P50
Isle of Man 1962-1966

Made for use on the Isle of Man, at 1.32 metres long the Peel P50 is one of the tiniest of microcars, with an equally small 49cc engine and three wheels. The Peel Engineering Company had already developed the Manxcar, but this was never taken to production— in fact fewer than 100 P50s were ever built. In 1965, the Peel Trident was introduced, a similarly petite three-wheeler with a plexiglass domed lid. By the time production had ended in 1965, something in the region of 50 Tridents had been produced.

Piaggio Ape

Italy 1948-the present Italy

Aeronautical engineer, Corradino D'Ascanio, designed the Vespa scooter in 1946. On seeing the design proposals, Piaggio's Managing Director, Enrico Piaggio, remarked that it looked like a wasp ('vespa').

In 1947, D'Ascanio started to develop the first Ape ('bee'), more or less a tricycle with handlebars, powered by a 125cc engine, and with a loading platform on the back. Practical, sturdy, economical and manoueverable, the Ape was embraced as both an urban and rural commercial vehicle when it arrived on the market and, because of this, acquired a reputation as both chic and hard-working. It was adopted in countries from Germany to India.

The Ape has undergone many modifications over the years, accompanied by an equally wide range of model names. Other similarly styled rivals joined the market. Ubiquitous in cities, towns and villages across Italy, its popularity continues. In November 2002, the most recent version of the Ape 50 went on sale.

Piaggio Ape 50, circa 1996.

Piaggio Ape 50, circa 1996.

Reliant Regal Mark I-VI
UK 1952-1962

British mainstay, Reliant, produced commercial vehicles before the war. The Regal was launched in 1952, initially for just over £400/$680. Like its competitor, the Bond Minicar range, the Regal went through many improvements, from I to VI, as a means of sustaining a competitive position in the small car marketplace. These modifications ranged from more sophisticated styling, including changes to the front grille and the introduction of a hard top, to increased driver and passenger space and comfort, and a higher specification of such features as windscreen wipers and indicators.

In order to keep up with the, by then, tough competition, Reliant launched, in 1962, the Regal 3/25 with its new, sharper styling, a range of colours and a host of added accessories from which to choose. The Regal 3/25 Super followed in 1965 and the 3/30 in 1968.

New models were added to the Reliant range, including the Robin. The company's reliability, tenacity and ability to adapt to changes have earned Reliant a respected place in the small car market.

In 1969, Reliant bought Bond Cars Ltd and, in 1970, produced the three-wheeled, orange Bond Bug.

"Not only does it afford comfort and weather protection superior to that of any extant motorcycle but–just as important–it offers economy and performance to match, and even surpass, many sidecar outfits, together with a seemingly inexhaustible capacity for hard work."[57]
Motor Cycling

Reliant Regal Mark VI, 1961.

Reliant Regal Super, circa 1965.

Reliant Regal 3/25, circa 1962.

room for a family of four

with ample luggage space

economical

family

motoring

Rovin D2
France 1946-1961

Rovin, late 1940s.

The French government encouraged the development of economy cars, the 'motocar', to get the nation moving again after the war. Naturally, a low purchase price and cheap maintenance were essential. The first 1946 Rovin D2 had a spot-welded steel body with no doors (driver and passenger stepping over its low sides to get in). As production grew, the initial 260cc engine was replaced by a larger, 425cc version. The Rovin's French contemporaries included the Renault 4CV and Citroën 2CV—all of which were exhibited in the 'minicar' sections of early post war Salons. Built by brothers Robert and Raoul Rovin, producers of cyclecars and motorcycles in France during the 1920s, the Rovin attracted a great deal of publicity. In the UK, *Autocar*, whilst describing it as a "neat little two-seater", also likened it to a dodgem car.[58]

In the region of 200 D2s were sold in the car's first year of production, after which the newer models, the D3 and D4, more sophisticated in design and manufacture, were introduced. However, it could not compete with its contemporaries and manufacture of the Rovin ended in 1961. In total, more than 1,000 Rovins were produced.

Scootacar De Luxe, 1960.

Scootacar (Mark 1) and De Luxe (Mark 2)
UK 1958-1965

Built in Leeds in the UK, the fibreglass Scootacar's characteristic shape resulted from the way in which the component parts were brought together. It is said that Henry Brown, producer of the Scootacar "sketched the outline of a Villiers 9E two-stroke engine with himself seated directly above it, and fitted everything else around".[59] Production of the Mark I (known simply as the Scootacar until the advent of the Scootacar De Luxe) began in 1957—the Mark 2, the De Luxe, was launched in 1960. Overall production ended in 1965, after the manufacture of about 1,500 cars.

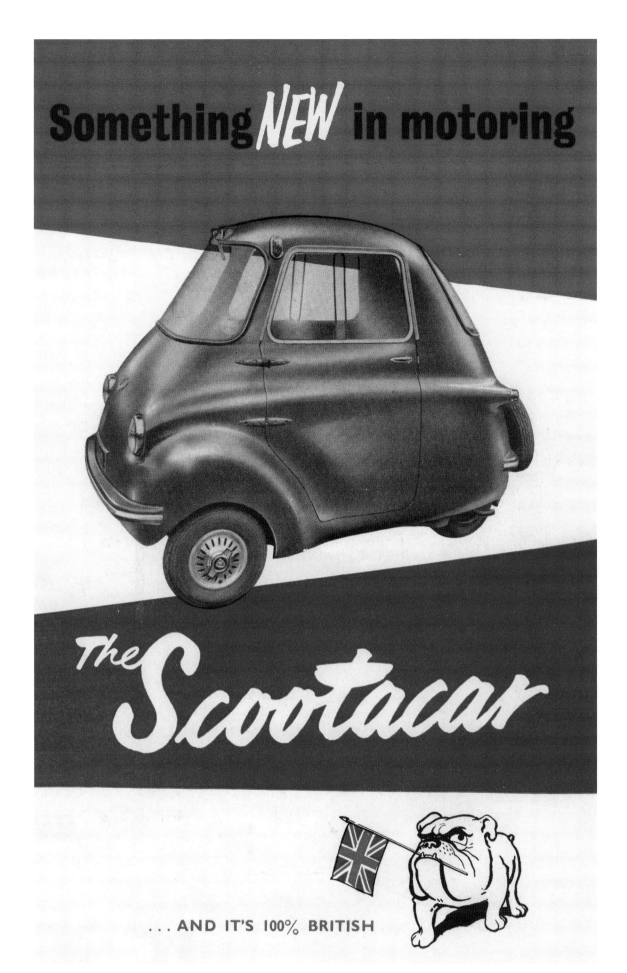

Scootacar, 1958.

Sinclair C5
UK 1985

In 1985, but with an eye far into the future, Sir Clive Sinclair introduced the now infamous Sinclair C5 to a general public not yet aware of the growing environmental problems associated with rapidly increasing traffic levels. In 1980, the UK government had abolished motor tax for electric vehicles; the battery powered C5 was developed to meet the new legislation and to address the increasing concerns in the UK and beyond about fuel reserves. The first truly mass produced electric vehicle, the C5 was intended to take its place as one of a range of economic and non-polluting vehicles; instead its commercial failure remains an enduring symbol in the UK's collective memory of tireless endeavour and a concept ahead of its time. Happily, the C5 has a large number of committed devotees and Sir Clive continues to produce electric vehicles: in the 1980s, the Zike, the 1990s the Zeta and a new car still to come.

Sinclair C5, 1985.

Smart

Germany 1998-the present

Since its launch in 1998, the Smart has established itself firmly as the reference point for the twenty-first century microcar, whilst embracing many of the earliest microcar values. Smart marketing has emphasised the car as an essential element of a contemporary design-conscious lifestyle, and has continued to align it with other products associated with design quality; in 2004, a limited edition model was offered complete with integrated i-pod. With the Smart now available in many countries around the world, its American launch, planned for 2006, has raised questions as to whether, even now, the United States is ready for a small car. Despite this, concerns about SUVs in the same market indicate that many Americans are ready to embrace some of the qualities that small car ownership can bring.

At 2.5 metres long and with a turning circle of 8.7 metres, an engine size of less than 700cc and a welcome attention to design detail, as well as safety, good fuel economy (with 3.78 litres of petrol lasting almost 100km), a network of retailers making for easy maintenance and prices starting at around £6,000/£10,200, the Smart has set the benchmark for contemporary small car ownership.

... the Smart has set the benchmark for contemporary small car ownership.

Subaru 360
Japan 1958-1971

In 1955, as a response to increasing traffic congestion, the K-class or *Kei-jidosha* was introduced in Japan as the smallest category of car by size and specification. As the category became more established, manufacturers developed new and innovative designs to satisfy the government's restrictions and make the most of the advantages that the category offered, including tax benefits and fewer parking restrictions. Produced from 1958 until the early 1970s, the Subaru 360's low price helped to ensure its popularity in Japan, however it did not transfer easily to the United States, where it was poorly received.

Subaru 360, 1970. Lane Motor Museum. Photo: David Yando.

PERFECT IN TOWN

Fascinating everywhere

BRILLIANT ON THE ROAD

Vespa 400, circa 1960.

L'Action Automobile et Touristique, October 1957.

Vespa 400
France 1957-1961

The four-wheeled Vespa 400 (Vespacar in the United States) was launched at the 1957 Paris Motor Show and, despite competing in the European microcar market against manufacturers including Fiat and Goggomobil, more than 30,000 Vespa 400s were sold between 1957 and 1961.

"Although its ancestry is different, it is easy to see the car as a successor to the Topolino designed in pre war days (itself an Italian conception), in providing up-to-date transport and a combination of useful performance with real economy. Others have attempted the same formula; the majority with far less success."[60]
Motor

Vespa 400, late 1950s.

Zündapp Janus, 1957.

The Cars   The Macro World of Microcars

Zündapp Janus, 1957.

Zündapp Janus
Germany 1957-1958

The most recognisable characteristic of the Janus was the fact that driver and front seat passenger faced forwards, while the two back seat passengers faced backwards; entry and exit is via a door at each end of the car. The symmetry simplified manufacture by minimising the number of pressings. Manufactured in Germany, the Zündapp Janus was launched at the 1957 Frankfurt Motor Show. The car was named after the Roman god Janus, who, with two faces back to back, each looking in opposite directions, is the god of beginnings and the guardian of gates and doors. The Zündapp is 3.1 metres long with a 248cc engine.

endnotes

1 The BMW 600 was known in the USA as the Isetta 600; elsewhere it was simply the BMW 600.

2 Herbert, Mark F, *Bubble Cars: A Concise History*, Edinburgh: M F Herbert, 1997.

3 see Marshall, Tony, *Microcars*, Stroud: Sutton Publishing Ltd, 1999, pp. 103-109.

4 Sparke, Penny, *A Century of Car Design*, London: Mitchell Beazley, 2002, p. 8.

5 Sparke, *Century*, p. 10.

6 Bayley, Stephen, *Moving Objects: 30 years of vehicle design at the Royal College of Art*, London: Eye-Q, 1999, p. 23.

7 Woodham, Jonathan M, *Twentieth Century Design*, Oxford: Oxford University Press, 1997, p. 115.

8 Sparke, *Century*, pp.17-22.

9 Ford, General Motors and Chrysler.

10 Agul, Vince, "Too Little, Too Soon", *Road and Track*, January 1975, p.79.

11 Agul, "Too Little", p. 78.

12 Bond Minicars from Mark C onwards.

13 "How much can you do without?", *Autocar*, 5 September 1952.

14 "BMW Isetta Road Test", *Autocar*, 4 November 1955.

15 *Motor Cycling*, 8 September 1955.

16 *Motor Cycling*, 27 September 1956.

17 In a feature called "Pint size and less", 4 January 1957, *Autocar* was at pains to point out that "The consumption figures quoted in the data which follow are [thus] rather loose, and even a change in wind speed and direction can play havoc with both economy and performance".

18 "How much can you do without?", *Autocar*, 5 September 1952.

19 *Motor Cycling*, 8 September 1955.

20 *Autocar*, 14 September 1956.

21 "Berkeley Sports Road Test", *Autocar*, 24 May 1957.

22 "The BMW Isetta 300", *Motor*, 13 March 1957.

23 "The BMW Isetta Coupe", *Motor Sport*, April 1956.

24 "The BMW 600 Road Test", *Motor*, 10 December 1958.

25 "The Bug", *Motor*, 6 June 1970.

26 "Three-wheeled funabout", *Motor*, 6 June 1970.

27 *Autocar*, 2 December 1955.

28 *Motor Cycling*, 30 April 1959.

29 Agul, "Too Little". p. 78.

30 Agul, "Too Little". p. 79.

31 Agul, "Too Little". p. 79.

32 Grayson, Stan, "Crosley of Cincinnati", *Automobile Quarterly*, Volume 16, Number 1, quoting an interview with Powel Crosley by James W Beckman in the *Cincinnati Enquirer*.

33 "The Fiat 500", *Lightcar*, 13 November 1936.

34 "Fiat 500 Convertible Road Test", *Autocar*, 27 November 1936.

35 "The Fiat 500 drop-head saloon", *The Motor*, 30 November 1937.

36 "How much can you do without?", *Autocar*, 5 September 1952.

37 The 1936 Topolino was followed by the 500B and 500C; the 600 was then introduced in 1955 before the Nuova 500 in 1957.

38 The Autocar Road Tests: Fiat 600 Saloon, *Autocar*, 13 May 1955

39 *Car*, May 2004.

40 "A New Topolino", *Autocar*, 5 July 1957.

41 "Fiat 500", *Autocar*, 1958.

42 "Fiat Giardiniera", *Autocar*, 17 February 1961.

43 "Meadows Frisky", *Autocar*, 1958.

44 The Australian Zeta Sport built by Lightburn was based on the Frisky Sprint.

45 "The Goggomobil", *Autosport*, 7 December 1956.

46 "The Goggomobil Regent 300 saloon", *Autosport*, 16 December 1960.

47 "The Heinkel Cabin Cruiser", *Motor*, 25 February 1957.

48 "Three-wheelers", *Motor Cycle*, 21 November 1963.

49 see Marshall, Tony, *Microcars*, for a description of the pre and post war UK Lloyd.

50 Wilkins, Gordon, "The Lloyd Alexander", *Sports Car and Lotus Owner*, 1957.

51 *Autocar*, 1958.

52 "Lloyd LP600 Road Test", *Autocar*, 1958.

53 For the story of the Fuldamobil, see Marshall, Tony, *More Microcars*, Stroud: Sutton Publishing Ltd, 2001.

54 For a great piece of film of L'Oeuf, go to http://www.ina.fr/voir_revoir/guerre/france/43-23.fr.html

55 "The Unicar Road Test", *Top Gear*, 1958.

56 "The Opperman Stirling", *The Motor*, 22 October 1958.

57 "Reliant 'Regal'", *Motor Cycling*, 4 October 1956.

58 "New French Model", *Autocar*, 4 October 1946.

59 Marshall, 1999, p. 97.

60 "The Vespa 400 de Luxe", *The Motor*, 1958.

Chapter Four
Thinking Small

thinking small

Aixam 500, 1999 © Aixam-Mega.

As we have seen, the original microcar had a brief but eventful history. The 1950s were its heydays; the 1960s its swan song; and the two following decades were the wilderness years during which time it all but disappeared from view, reappearing occasionally as a nostalgic memento of times past or an oddity like the Sinclair C5. But since the mid-1990s, microcars have begun to raise their heads above the parapet again. Today we have the ubiquitous Smart, the Microcar Virgo, Ligier Ambra 505, Aixam 500 and many more. And even the Reliant Robin is nudging its way back with a new 848cc engine, fibreglass body with sleeker styling and light-reactive paint. So what has brought about the microcar resurgence today?

Jos Darling of Bath University is the engineer of the 1 metre-wide 'Clever', a tilting three-wheeler, which is due for production in 2005. He says that "the increase in traffic in our towns and cities means that we have to find a way to make our vehicles smaller". Darling suggests—appearing to proclaim his invention as part of the new dawn of microcars—that "the advent of microcars (sic!) is a… search for a small vehicle to get around cities".[1] His modish Compact Low Emission Vehicle for Urban Transport (Clever) begs several questions. Firstly, why can't scientists come up with realistic acronyms? Secondly, do we really need or want smaller cars? But most importantly, what does the new generation of microcars—and the culture that gives rise to them—bode for the future?

If traffic continues to build but the infrastructure refuses to expand, soon we will have to be crammed into even more miniature vehicles

The suggestion that small city cars are a way of beating traffic gridlock is undoubtedly logical in its own terms. For a given length of road, if traffic volumes increase—as they are projected to do—then gridlock will eventually ensue. Consequently, the smaller the car, the more vehicles that can be fitted along its length. But is this Malthusian equation legitimate? If so, then the latest generation of small cars can only be a temporary solution: if traffic continues to build but the infrastructure refuses to expand, soon we will have to be crammed into even more miniature vehicles with our knees tucked tightly under our chins, to ensure that we manage to be congestion-free for a few years more.

Ligier Be Up, 2004 © Ligier Automobiles.

As the Ministry for Transport pointed out in its influential 1967 report, little research had been conducted on driving behaviour but that "length alone is not very important in determining the amount of roadspace a vehicle needs when on the move and its importance diminishes as speed increases."[2] This is because the length of the car becomes a less significant percentage of the stopping distance (the overall space required by any vehicle) at faster speeds.

But contemporary demand management policy argues that we should reduce the quantum of cars on the roads in the first place; not just the size of the vehicle. This is intended to buy us yet more time but actually stems from a wanton misinterpretation of a UK government report which made the phrase "more roads lead to more traffic" into an orthodoxy.[3] If then, more roads leads to more cars, then closing roads some say, will lead to fewer cars.[4] QED. The idea that we should maybe increase the infrastructure is now parodied as a comically out-dated notion. Microcars are undoubtedly an embodiment of reducing the impact that driving has on the natural world within the parameters of the existing infrastructure. However, at least the modern microcar recognises that personal mobility is a good thing. But only just. Regardless of the size of vehicle, very few people these days think that driving more is something to be encouraged.

MC1 from Microcar.

In the 1960s, 'predict and provide' was as hip as 'peace and love'.

Grecav EKE 2000, aluminum frame.

Transport policy today has less to do with getting from A to B quickly and efficiently, and more about the ethical dilemmas involved in wanting to go to B in the first place.

The 1963 Buchanan Report *Traffic in Towns* has subsequently been claimed by environmentalists to have fired the first critical shot across the bows of urban car use.[5] Famously, Colin Buchanan described the car as a "monster of great potential destructiveness"– but in fact, his report was one of the first attempts to look rationally at the requirements for sensibly accommodating car-based traffic in our towns and cities. Lest we forget, Buchanan's report advocated a pedestrian-free six-lane high-speed roadway down Oxford Street! This pro-road penchant should not be too surprising given that the Buchanan Report was published in 1963 by a Conservative government simultaneously employing Baron Beeching to slash the railway system in recognition that road transport was the only way forward, effectively marking the official end of the Steam Age. Remarkably prescient, the Buchanan Report–as did Beeching's axe–had a progressive edge to its negative projections. Both were brutal and heavy handed, but both demanded more road infrastructure to ensure that the speed of mobility was preserved, nurtured and improved upon. In the 1960s, 'predict and provide' was as hip as 'peace and love'.

Even when, in 1967, the Ministry of Transport reported that "planning and highway solutions alone cannot cope with all our traffic problems", they continued in their belief that "they are by far the most important factors in resolving our traffic congestion".[6] Astutely, the same report goes on to emphasise the need for segregation amongst transport modes (something which wasn't acted upon in the UK but has been achieved in those continental European countries that planners now hold up as exemplary green transport schemes). Apart from the dated appearance of the UK government's 1960s design-by-committee solutions, their ideas for elevated highways transporting compact city-cars at 40mph were positive infrastructural responses to congestion. 40 years later and most city traffic averages a heady 11mph. Even the pseudo-futuristic-looking micro-pods of the ULTra suspended rail network aspire only to 25mph.

Cars in Cities concludes by saying that "in assessing the relative attractiveness of different proportions of public and private transport, weight should be given to making it possible for people to do what they want".[7] Those were the days. The belief in technical solutions often reflects the can-do mood at any given time. Unfortunately, for all the technical and high-tech talk today, we seem to live in a *no-can-do* society. Techno-fixes are frowned upon (if they encourage consumption and use too many resources) and instead of doing what we want, we are enjoined to do what is best. Transport policy today has less to do with getting from A to B quickly and efficiently, and more about the ethical dilemmas involved in wanting to go to B in the first place. Modern microcars are an attempt to address the moral impasse: to emotionally relate to the intractability of congestion and one's place within it, while wanting a nippy run-about to dodge the worst of it?

Most people recognise that renouncing the convenience of modern mobility altogether would be an eccentric thing to do. The Mitsuoka MC-1 one-person buggy with a 50cc air-cooled engine will remain, I would wager, a minority interest vehicle. Alongside the mainstream of Smart cars or Nissan's Micromini, these microcars seem to exhibit what Bryan Appleyard describes as "one 'me' generation succeed (ing) another, each convinced that it had found the meaning of life in the pursuit of self-realisation".[8] Buying small, is doing your bit. "(Today) there is... only... the refusal not to sell your self."[9] A sense of charity in a fragmented world. But doing your bit for the environment might be a dubious claim given the lack of efficiency in the small-scale production runs that these new vehicles demand—especially since reducing consumption is the philosophical basis for their production in the first place).[10]

In an article in *The Independent* about the 2004 New York Motor Show, entitled *Forget eco-friendly: New York is thinking big* Alistair Weaver argues that "there is little incentive for people to run ecologically friendly cars and for all the manufacturers' eco-posturing, the (US) market continues to be dominated by SUVs and gargantuan pick-up trucks."[11] But this misses the point. As two leading urbanists say, "the policy of pushing back cars and giving urban life better conditions continues to be a European phenomenon primarily, but it is interesting to note that corresponding urban policy strategies can now be found in cities in North and South America, Asia and Australia".[12] Even in the US—the country parodied as eschewing the green revolution—environmental standards still dictate the terms of the global debate. Look no further than Hollywood (an institution premised on predicting the next Big Thing) and its simultaneous global launch of the environmental disaster movie, *The Day After Tomorrow*, 2004. It may be called, in some quarters, 'free-trade environmentalism', but the United States buys into it—even in the breach. Influential ecologists such as William McDonagh are principal advisors to Nike, Ford and GM, while Amory Lovins, another eminent ecologist, has been ranked as the 22nd most powerful person in the global automotive industry by *Car Magazine*. Apparently, even William Clay Ford Jr has called for higher fuel taxes—his attempt to seem as corporately socially responsible—in a bid to reduce the impact of his own production of larger vehicles and to bolster the new market for hybrid small cars.[13] The fact that the rest of the world, in registering their compliance with Kyoto, is building small cars to comply with the energy-saving, reduced-impact ethos is no different to the debate governing US auto-manufacturing more generally. On one hand we have small cars flaunting their smallness; on the other hand, we have big cars thinking small. There is a fine line differentiating the two.

SAM, 2001 © CREE Ltd.

Even in the US—the country parodied as eschewing the green revolution—environmental standards still dictate the terms of the global debate.

Toyota PM Concept 2003 © Toyota GB.

Grecav EKE, 2000 crash test.

Pasquali 'Elettricitta' riscio electrico.

In political terms, if motoring is charged with a range of ills—from obesity to community breakdown, from sloth to isolationism, from local pollution to global warming, from individual stress to the death of children—what positive thing is it that car manufacturers represent?

At the Detroit Motor Show in January 2003, Ford unveiled the Model U (one letter up on Laurel & Hardy's Model T). It is a sizeable family car but has an 'impact' of a far smaller car. This concept car's new technology will include hydrogen fuel cells, be built from recyclable materials and be lubricated by sunflower seed oil. These are so-called benign technologies that are deemed not to affect the balance of nature, or better, of a concept of nature as a static entity completely disengaged from any human action. Not surprisingly, many involved in environmentalism laud the growth of global stewardship and the fact that certain businesses are buying into it.

Ben Hunt, author of *The Timid Corporation: Why Business is Terrified of Taking Risk*, argues: "As corporations try hard to reduce their apparently negative impact, new problems are created. For one thing, they make bad decisions based on dogma rather than common sense. Since it is not clear exactly why corporations are having a negative impact, or behaving irresponsibly, it is not clear why they can make a difference by acting responsibly."[14] Companies such as Ford, for all their SUV bravado or for the ecological transformation of their Rouge Center—Ford's attempt to reconcile natural and industrial systems into both a productive and regenerative, landscape—are wracked with self-doubt, as are practically all manufacturers. In political terms, if motoring is charged with a range of ills—from obesity to community breakdown, from sloth to isolationism, from local pollution to global warming, from individual stress to the death of children—what positive thing is it that car manufacturers represent?[15] Political and transport commentator Christian Wolmar has noted that "another often forgotten effect is the sheer slaughter of wildlife on the roads. From frogs and sparrows to badgers and herons....There is a daily massacre on our roads."[16] Presumably, drivers of the new Omni Electrolite can satisfy themselves that with such a lightweight vehicle, a cane toad might have a 50:50 chance of coming off best.

In France, flax and hemp are being used as environmentally-friendly panelising materials (by Techni-Lin in Normandy and Effireal in the Maine-et-Loire region respectively).[17] Alan Crosky of the School of Material Science and Engineering in the University of New South Wales in Australia says of his rhetorically-loaded car made out of elephant grass, that "the lighter the car, the less fuel you need to propel it".[18] This is something that Amory Lovins has been working on in relation to the hyper-car, at his Rocky Mountain Institute for many years.[19] Solar panels are suited to powering petrol stations more so than cars, but the economic-efficiency of photovoltaic panels will inevitably become a feature of low-level in-car electricity production. From the ubiquitous hydrogen-fuel cell to bio-diesel to California-based Flywheel Systems (a clockwork car), fascinating and potentially efficient though all of these inventions and discoveries are, it is worth understanding what the underlying philosophy is that has propelled them into mainstream production.[20] It is also important to recognise their place within the pervasive culture of limits within Western societies today.

The CLEVER (Compact Low Emission Vehicle for Urban Transport) vehicle will run on natural gas and is expected to be completed in 2005.

So-called experimentation in green technologies such as hydrogen power, fuel cell technologies and non-petroleum based propulsion is fine as far as it goes, but because of a moralistic climate that says that anything other than renewables is somehow harmful to the planet, experimentation is being funnelled into a narrowly defined area of 'responsible' research. Hydrogen power is indeed a much-needed advance on gratuitous gas-guzzlers because it is more efficient—a clear improvement in terms of a straightforward cost-benefit appraisal of outputs to inputs—but by putting all of our eggs into this one basket, we may be missing out on other more inventive, productive means of fuelling our vehicles. A *New Scientist* editorial predicts that hydrogen will become the mainstream energy source in 50 years while James Randerson says that "hydrogen fuel cells, even though they are not commercially viable, are… our only realistic alternative to the petrol engine".[21] But since much of the debate is about whether—not *how*—we should travel, it is hardly surprising that promoting better methods of fuelling cars is deemed by some to be pointless. Mayer Hillman, Emeritus Professor at the Policy Studies Institute, and arch green campaigner says, "people say technology will solve the problem, for instance, by making more efficient use of fuel, and I say no—if you don't reduce demand first, then by making it more efficient you'll increase demand for it".[22] It is precisely because we have reduced our horizons that, today, size is important. The primary difference then, between the first generation microcars and today's citycars, is ambition and a belief in the project of increasing and improving mobility for as many people as possible. Today, there is no such clarity of purpose. Indeed, Hillman predicts that "the day will come when people in the street will feel sorry for someone passing in a car".[23]

For some, the appellation 'microcar' is now deemed to include tricycles and quadracycles: covered chasses similar to Omni's Electrolite or the Twike, powered by solar panels, battery packs and often with back-up pedal generators. A wind-up radio on wheels. The Corbin Sparrow is an electric retro-Messerschmitt-cum-Reliant Robin. These are low-to-zero emission vehicles, use minimal materials and tick all of the right boxes (Ford's 2004 Focus, while not being, in any shape or form, a microcar, has labelled its Duratec 2.3 litre engine as a "*partial* zero emission vehicle"!).

But by putting all of our eggs into this one basket, we may be missing out on other more inventive, productive means of fuelling our vehicles.

F 300 Life Jet, 1997 © Mercedes-Benz.

Carver, 2003, © Vandenbrink b.v.

Tonino Lamborghini's Town Life, Italy.

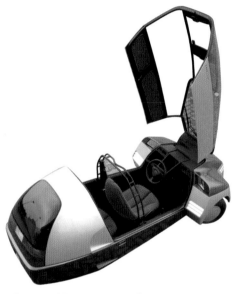

The TWIKE is an electric three-wheeler with supplemental peddle-power. In 1998, six Twikes set out from Bern, Switzerland on a trip that covered 15 countries and saw them reach Nord Cap, 320km north of the Arctic Circle, before going back to Bern. The 11,000km journey took 11 weeks and each vehicle completed the trip on 55kwh or $44/£26 worth of electricity. © TWIKE

Ghia Cockpit, 1981 © Ford Motor Company.

In August 2001, the European Commission awarded a three-year contract for the Cybercars project to develop a "new transport concept for the cities of tomorrow".[24] Cybercar projects include smart road guidance systems (such as Frog Navigation[25]) and tele-operated intelligent vehicles (Robosoft[26], etc.). In general, these are battery-powered and computer-managed by a distributed network control system, contain state of the art safety and navigation technology, and unfortunately seem to be modelled on the golfcart. Exciting though these ventures are, at the moment they are not intended as personal, but public, transport. But their aim to "reduce the use of traditional cars", is not the most magnanimous basis for a futuristic transport plan. Furthermore, their reliance on intelligent technologies, from satellite navigation to embedded sensor controls, is all that raises this new generation of vehicles from the level of glorified Thai tuk-tuks. Given that the enviro-logic tends towards dual power alternative technology vehicles (a power source with pedal-power back-up, etc.), maybe we are not far from seeing a mainstream return of the rickshaw.

Daihatsu Copen, 2003 © Daihatsu Vehicle Distributors Ltd.

The fact that some vehicle designs incorporate muscle-powered technologies more associated with developing nations is quite an indictment. But even high profile cyber-technology, in today's social framework can seem frightening rather than liberating, instinctively reinforcing certain anti-development instincts. Susan Greenfield, neuroscientist and director of the Royal Institution of Great Britain voices her more populist fears of future generations' reliance on robotic technology. Following Francis Fukuyama's lead, she dreads that humanity might lose something in the process. It is true, she says, that machines "may not be conscious, and they may not be hell-bent on world domination—but there is a clear threat that is just as sinister and certainly more likely."[27] This threat, she goes on to explain, includes the fact that as we relate to and rely on machines more and more, so we lose our ability to relate to other humans, condemning us to an 'autistic' future.[28] Unfortunately, she proposes no vision other than doubt. Interesting maybe, but not exactly helpful. Historically, worry has not been the best driver for technological advance.

While the *New Scientist* argues that "technology has a life of its own", the dynamic within society is the best guide to how quickly and how successfully those technologies will be taken up.[29] In the past, vehicles became cleaner, faster, more efficient, quieter and better—without the contemporary infatuation with regulatory constraints, an anti-car bias, environmental scare-mongering, or risk-aversion. Will the pervasive precautionary climate be a positive motivation for change or a drag on development? If human activity is seen as an automatic cause of environmental harm then what hope for human engineered technology to improve matters? Sir Martin Rees, Astronomer Royal, announces that unless we mend our ways, reduce our patterns of consumption, we have but 100 years to inhabit the planet before the wrath of Gaia shall befall us.[30] Repent ye! Yea, and there shall be a renting of bikes and a chattering of classes.

It is true that many people view the microcar as a nostalgic paeon to times past. And why not? The world has seen nothing like them since; a joyful expression of the liberating dream of mobility that allowed ordinary cash-strapped punters to buy into the car-owning democracy. We mustn't become too romantic about it (and there is nothing to be gained by going backwards) but in the 1950s and 1960s, travel was still celebrated as something that really did broaden the mind. This positive attitude to mobility is what we have to reclaim if the new generation of microcars is not to become a symbol and a victim of our age of uncertainty. The modern microcar has tremendous potential to become a boon for certain journeys and specific functions and to take its place alongside a range of transport options. It has the potential to become an economically efficient short-range car. But in order to fulfil this aspiration we first have to reject the idea that short-range journeys should be walked and not driven in the first place.

TH!NK city, 2003 © Think Nordic AS. Photo by Knut Bry/TinAgent.

Ligier Nova.

Some of the most successful first-generation microcars, designed and built to open up to a whole host of people the benefits of travel and mobility, had at their disposal far lower levels of the technology and manufacturing knowledge we have now. In many cases, their appearance too strengthened them as symbols of a new confidence. Their manufacturers, engineers and designers found ingenious solutions to problems encountered and, though there were difficulties associated with the majority of the cars, of greater or lesser severity, broadly they were welcomed with open arms and the problems were either overlooked or overcome.

Second time around, we have technology at our disposal of a far greater level of sophistication, within a changed social and political climate. Some examples of the new microcar generation are desirable in their own right, with slick, confident styling that does not need to wear its environmental credentials on its sleeve.

In essence, instead of big cars thinking small, it is the small car that should be thinking big, challenging the assumption that inadequate infrastructure will prevail and that it will have to fit into a bleakly congested world. It should not endorse the guilt that, simply because of its mere existence as a 'car', it is doing harm, but slightly less than a bigger car. It should not be seen as a cramped alternative to the bus. It should maintain high standards of design similar to those we have come to expect of a conventional small car. But, unless we can start to argue that mobility, infrastructure and personal private transport are a good thing, then microcars will have no *raison d'etre*. This would be an abrogation of the opportunity presented to us all to bring some speed, functionality, convenience, comfort and fun back into motoring, as only microcars can do. As such, significantly, it would destroy the ability of the second generation of microcars to carry the mantle of the first.

The Smart City Coupé © Smart.

endnotes

1   "Clever car to solve congestion", BBC News, 8 April 2004. see http://news.bbc.co.uk/1/hi/technology/3610083.stm

2   *Cars for Cities: A study of trends in the design of vehicles with particular reference to their use in towns*, Report of the Steering Group and Working Group, Ministry for Transport, London: HMSO, 1967, p. 13.

3   SACTRA (Standing Advisory Committee on Trunk Road Assessment) Report, 1992.

4   Cairns, S, Hass-Klau S and Goodwin PB, *Traffic Impact of Highway Capacity Reductions: Assessment of the Evidence*, London: Landor Publishing, 1998.

5   Buchanan, Colin, *Traffic in Towns: A study of the longterm problems of traffic in urban area*, London: HMSO, 1963.

6   *Cars for Cities*, p. vi.

7   *Cars for Cities*, p. viii.

8   Appleyard, Bryan, "Are You Sinning Comfortably?", *The Sunday Times Magazine*, 11 April 2004, p. 23.

9   Appleyard, "Sinning", p. 23.

10 "A totally new Japanese car requires 1.7 million hours of research and development time from blank sheet of paper to the first customer delivery. With an average run of one million cars, the design cost amortised across production run comes in at only $425/£250 per car, but each car has the benefit of 1.7 million hours of design thought." Michael Trudgeon, "Architecture as an anti-technological virus: the work of Michael Trudgeon", *World Architecture*, Issue 23, May 1993, quoted in Pawley, Martin, *Terminal Architecture*, London: Reaktion Books ,1998, p. 196.

11 Weaver, Alistair, "Forget eco-friendly: New York thinks big", *The Independent*,13 April 2004, p. 8.

12 Gehl, Jan and Gemzoe, Lars, *New City Spaces*, Copenhagen: The Danish Architectural Press, 2000.

13 McRae, Hamish, "Doom Time for the SUV", *The Independent*, 20 April 2004.

14 Hunt, Ben, "Concerned Companies", 14 April 2004, http://www.spiked-online.com/Articles/0000000CA4D2.htm.

15 David Engwicht, the originator of walking buses, says "I realized that one of the most insidious side effects of car-based transport systems was its contribution to segregation and the loss of social diversity". Engwicht, David, *Reclaiming Our Cities & Towns: Better Living with Less Traffic*, Philadelphia: New Society Publishers, 1993, p. 29.

16 Wolmar, Christian, "Unlocking the Gridlock: The Key to a New Transport Policy", Friends of the Earth Discussion Paper, 1997, p. 16.

17 "Hi-Tech Flax and Hemp—From Car Panels to Lightweight Concrete", French Technology Press Bureau, http://www.globalhemp.com/News/2004/March/high_tech_flax_and_hemp.php.

18 "Scientists Develop Car Parts From Hemp Grass", *National Geographic*, 6 June 2001, http://news.nationalgeographic.com/news/2001/06/0606_wirehemp.html.

19 Weizsacker, Ernst von, Lovins, Amory B and Lovins, L Hunter, "Factor Four: Doubling Wealth, Halving Resource Use—A Report to the Club of Rome", London: Earthscan, 1997.

20 Vidal, John, "Chip shops offer fat chance for fry-drive revolution", *The Guardian*, 21 October 2002.

21 "The Clean Green Energy Dream", Energy Special Report, *New Scientist*, 16 August 2003, p. 8.

22 Hillman, Mayer, quoted in "A Chain Reaction" by Anne Karpf, *The Guardian*, 2 November 2002.

23 Hillman quoted in Karpf.

24 "Cybercars on the Move", *Transport Matters*, August 2002.

25 The Frog (Free Ranging On Grid) technology is an Automated Guided Vehicle System (AGVS) that creates intelligent vehicles which navigate by means of electronic maps. see www.frog.nl.

26 Robosoft "develops and supplies advanced mobile robotics solutions for transport, Cleanliness and Research Applications". see www.robosoft.fr.

27 Greenfield, Susan, *Tomorrow's People: How 21st Century Technology Is Changing The Way We Think And Feel*, London: Allen Lane, 2003, p. 248.

28 Greenfield, *Tomorrow's*, pp. 78-79.

29 "Power Struggle: Everyone seems to want a hydrogen economy, we just can't agree what it is", *New Scientist*, 16 August 2003.

30 Rees, Martin, *Our Final Century: Will the Human Race Survive the Twenty-First Century?*, London: William Heinemann, 2003.

bibliography

Adeney, Martin, *The Motor Makers: The Turbulent History of the British Car Industry*, London: Fontana, 1988.

Albus, Volker, Kras, Reyer and Woodham, Jonathan, eds, *Icons of Design: The 20th Century*, London: Prestel, 2003.

Alder, Trevor, ed, *Bond Bug*, Ipswich: Transport Source Books Ltd, 1996.

Alder, Trevor, ed, *Bond Cars* (up to 1969), Ipswich: Transport Source Books Ltd, 1995.

Alder, Trevor, ed, *Microcar Volume 1*, Olney: Transport Source Books Ltd, 1992.

Alder, Trevor, ed, *Microcar Volume 2*, Olney: Transport Source Books Ltd, 1993.

Alder, Trevor, ed, *Microcar Volume 3*, Olney: Transport Source Books Ltd, 1993.

Alder, Trevor, ed, *Microcar Volume 4*, Ipswich: Transport Source Books Ltd, 1994.

Armstrong, Philip, Glyn, Andrew and Harrison, John, *Capitalism Since 1945*, Oxford: Basil Blackwell, 1991.

Banham, Reyner, *Theory and Design in the First Machine Age*, London: The Architectural Press, 1960.

Barker, T C, *The Economic and Social Effects of the Spread of Motor Vehicles*, London: Macmillan, 1987.

Batchelor, Dean, Poole, Chris and Robson, Graham, *The Great Book of Sportscars*, New York: Portland House, 1988.

Bayley, Stephen, *Harley Earl*, London: Trefoil Publications, 1990.

Bayley, Stephen, Garner, Philippe and Sudjic, Deyan, *Twentieth Century Style and Design*, New York: Van Nostrand Reinhold Company, 1986.

Bayley, Stephen and Chapman, Giles, eds, *Moving Objects: thirty years of vehicle design from the Royal College of Art*, London: Eye-Q Ltd, 1999.

Bayley, Stephen, *Sex, Drink and Fast Cars*, New York: Pantheon Books, 1986

Beaulieu, Lord Montagu of and Georgano, G N, *Early Days on the Road*, London: Michael Joseph, 1976.

Bell, Jonathan, ed, *Carchitecture: when the car and the city collide*, London: August, 2001.

Bell, Jonathan, *Concept Car Design: Driving the Dream*, Rotovision, 2003.

Bobbitt, Malcolm, *Bubblecars and Microcars*, Marlborough: The Crowood Press Ltd, 2003.

Bobbitt, Malcolm, *Those Were the Days*, Dorset: Veloce Publishing, 2003.

Borgeson, Griffith and Jaderquist, Eugene, *Sports and Classic Cars*, New York: Prentice-Hall, 1955.

Boyne, Walter, *Power Behind the Wheel: Creativity and the Evolution of the Automobile*, New York: Artabras, 1991.

Buchanan, C D, *Mixed Blessing: The Motor Car in Britain*, London: Leonard Hill, 1958.

Burkhart, Bryan & Hunt, David, *Airstream: The History of the Land Yacht*, San Francisco: Chronicle Books, 2000.

Bush, Donald J, *The Streamlined Decade*, New York: George Braziller, 1975.

Clarke, R M, *Fiat 500 Gold Portfolio 1936-1972*, Cobham: Brooklands Books Ltd, 1994.

Clarke, R M, *Goggomobil Royal, Dart, Regent*, Cobham: Brooklands Books Ltd, 1996.

Clarke, R M, *Isetta Gold Portfolio 1953-1964*, Cobham: Brooklands Books Ltd, 1997.

Clarke, R M, *Messerschmitt Gold Portfolio 1954-1964*, Cobham: Brooklands Books Ltd.

Church, R, *The Rise and Decline of the British Motor Industry: Studies in Economic and Social History*, London: Macmillan, 1994.

Crawford, J H, *Carfree Cities*, Utrecht: International Books, 2000.

Davis, S C H, *Cars cars cars cars*, London: Paul Hamlyn, 1967.

Deanborn, M I, *Streamlining America*, Detroit: Henry Ford Museum, 1986.

Demaus, A B, *Motoring in the Twenties and Thirties*, London: Batsford, 1979.

Dregni, Michael and Dregni, Eric, *Scooters!*, Osceola, FL: Motorbooks International, 1995.

Flink, J J, *The Car Culture*, Cambridge: MIT Press, 1975.

Foreman-Peck, J, Bowden, S and McKinlay, A, *The British Motor Industry*, Manchester: Manchester University Press, 1995.

Forty, Adrian, *Objects of Desire*, London: Thames and Hudson, 1986.

Fukuyama, Francis, *The Great Disruption: Human nature and the reconstruction of social order*, London: Profile Books Ltd, 1999.

Gagnon, Jacques, *Guide des Voitures Anciennes: Les modèles préferés des Québécois*, Montréal: Les Éditions de l'Hommes Canada, 1997.

Girardet, Herbert, *The Gaia Atlas of Cities*, London: Gaia Books Ltd, 1996.

Hall, Peter and Ward, Colin, *Sociable Cities: The Legacy of Ebenezer Howard*, Indianapolis: John Wiley & Sons, 1998.

Henslowe, L, *Buying a Car?*, London: Hutchinson, 1930.

Herbert, Mark F, *Bubble Cars: A Concise History*, Edinburgh: M F Herbert, 1997.

Heskett, John, *Industrial Design*, London: Thames and Hudson, 1980.

Hill, Ken, *Three-Wheelers (Shire Album 165)*, Princes Risborough: Shire Publications Ltd, 1986.

Hillier, Beris, *The Style of the Century*, New York: Watson-Guptill Publications, 1998

Jodard, Paul, *Raymond Loewy*, London: Trefoil Publications, 1992.

Kenney, Martin and Florida, Richard, *Beyond Mass Production: The Japanese System and its Transfer to the US*, Oxford: Oxford University Press, 1993.

Kessel, Adrienne, *The World's Strangest Automobiles*, Philadelphia: Chelsea House Publishers, 1998.

Künnecke, Otto and Schweitzer, Andy, *Kleinschnittger: Wirtschaftswunder im Kleinformat*, Wallmoden: Bodensteiner Verlag, 1999.

Landry, Charles, *The Creative City*, London: EarthScan, 2000.

Lerner, Steve, ed, *Beyond the Earth Summit: Conversations with advocates of Sustainable Development*, Bolinas: Commonweal, 1992.

Lichtenstein, Claude and Engler, Franz, eds, *Streamlined: A Metaphor for Progress—The Esthetics of Minimal Drag*, trans. B Hauss-Fitton and M Robinson, Baden: Lars Müller Publishers, 1995.

Margolis, Ivan, *Automobiles by Architects*, Chichester: Wiley-Academy, 2000.

Marshall, Tony, *Microcars*, Stroud: Sutton Publishing Ltd, 2000.

Marshall, Tony, *More Microcars*, Stroud: Sutton Publishing Ltd, 2001.

Mazzanti, Sassa and Ornella, Davide, *Vespa: Italian Street Style*, Florence: Scriptum Editions, 2003.

McShane, C, *Down the Asphalt Path: The Automobile and the American City*, New York: Columbia University Press, 1994.

Meyhöfer, Dirk, *motortecture*, Ludwigsburg: avedition, 2003.

Motte, Nel & Peter, *Balkan Roads to Istanbul*, London: Robert Hale Ltd, 1960.

Newbury, Stephen, *The Car Design Yearbook 1: The Definitive Guide to New Concept and Production Cars Worldwide*, London, Merrell Publishers Ltd, 2002.

Newbury, Stephen, *The Car Design Yearbook 2: The Definitive Guide to New Concept and Production Cars Worldwide*, London, Merrell Publishers Ltd, 2003.

Plowden, W, *The Motor Car and Politics in Britain*, Harmondsworth: Pelican Books, 1976.

Prizer, Vernon, *The Irrepressible Automobile*, New York and Toronto: McLelland and Stewart, 1986.

Pulos, Arthur J, *The American Design Adventure*, Cambridge, MA: MIT Press, 1988

Rees, Chris, *Microcar Mania: The Definitive History of the Small Car*, Minster Lovell and New Yatt: Bookmarque Publishing, 1995.

Richardson, K, *The British Motor Industry 1896-1939: A Social and Economic History*, London: Macmillan, 1977.

Robinson, Heath and Browne K R G, *How to Be a Motorist*, London: Duckworth, 1939.

Robinson, Heath and Browne K R G, *How to Live in a Flat*, London: Duckworth, 1936.

Rogers, Richard, *Cities for a Small Planet*, London: Faber and Faber, 1997.

Rogers, Richard and Power, Anne, *Cities for a Small Country*, London: Faber and Faber, 2000.

Sedgewick, M, *Cars of the 1930s*, London: BT Batsford Ltd, 1970.

Sedgwick, Michael, *Cars of the 1930s*, London: BT Batsford Ltd, 1970.

Sedgwick, Michael, *The Motor Car 1946-56*, London: BT Batsford Ltd, 1978.

Setright, L J K, Drive On! *A Social History of the Motor Car*, London: Granta, 2003.

Shacket, Sheldon R, T*he Complete Book of Electric Vehicles*, London: Millington Books, 1980.

Siuri, Bill, *Micro and Mini Car Buyer's Guide*, Osceola, FL: Motorbooks International, 1995.

Sparke, Penny, *A Century of Car Design*, London: Mitchell Beazley, 2002.

Sparrow, Andrea and Sparrow, David, *More! Bubblecars and Microcars: Colour Family Album*, Dorchester: Veloce Publishing, 1997.

Springer, Anthony M, ed, *Aerospace Design: Aircraft, Spacecraft and the Art of Modern Flight*, London: Merrell Publishers Ltd, 2003.

Sutton, R, *Motor Mania: Stories from a Motoring Century*, London: Collins and Brown, 1996.

Thirlby, David, *Minimal Motoring: From Cyclecar to Microcar*, Stroud: Tempus Publishing Ltd, 2002.

Thyssen Bornemissza, Peter von, *Die Grosse Enzyklopädie Der Kleinen Automobile–Europäische Kleinwagen 1945-1955* Frankfurt: Zyklam Verlag 1989.

Thorold, Peter, *The Motoring Age: The Automobile and Britain 1896-1939*, London: Profile Books, 2003.

Topham, Sean, *Where's My Space Age: The Rise and Fall of Futuristic Design*, London: Prestel, 2003.

Tracey, H, *Father's first car*, Chatham: Routledge and Kegan Paul, 1966.

Williamson, Judith, *Decoding Advertisements: Ideology and Meaning in Advertising*, London: Marion Boyars Publishers Ltd, 1978.

Wollen, Peter and Kerr, Joe, *Autopia: Cars and Culture*, London, Reaktion Books Ltd, 2002.

Woodham, Jonathan M, *Twentieth Century Design*, Oxford: Oxford University Press, 1997.

Worthington-Williams, M, *From Cyclecar to Microcar*, London: Beaulieu Books/Dalton Watson, 1981.

Zeichner, W, *Kleinwagen International*, Gerlingen: Bleicher, 1990.

BMW Isetta und Ihre Konkurrenten 1955-62, Munich: Schrader Automobil-Bucher, 1986.

Cars for Cities: *A study of trends in the design of vehicles with particular reference to their use in towns*, London: HMSO, 1967.

Microcars, Hockley: Unique Motor Books, 2001.

articles

Barlow, Jason, "Relive that Monte Carlo magic, when our Mini beat the world", *The Independent*, 17 February 2004.

Boase, Tessa, "Car Design: the dawn of a new age", *Telegraph Motoring*, 22 November 2003.

Bremner, Richard, "A Tale of Two Dynasties", *Management Today*, January 2004.

Hebdige, Dick, "Object as Image: The Italian Scooter Cycle", *Block 5*, 1981.

Higgs, Don, "Bubbles that never burst", *Weekend Telegraph*, 23 October 1993.

Schofield, Jack, "Emotional about design", *The Guardian*, 11 March 2004.

Sewell, Brian, "The 'Little Mouse' that roared with Italian chic", *The Independent*, 9 March 2004.

Webster, Ben, "It's the green, clean, family-friendly machine that manufacturers tell us is the future of motoring", *The Times*, 6 January 2004.

Whittell, Giles, "The clean, green car out in front is a Toyota", *The Times*, 9 January 2004.

"Microcar mania for rising bubble tops", *Classic Car Weekly*, 12 March 1997.

"The bubbles blow into Britain", *The Times*, 11 January 1997.

selected owners clubs and their websites

(in the UK unless otherwise stated)
Most of the clubs not listed here can be found through links from the sites below.

A to Z of three-wheelers
www.3wheelers.com

Berkeley
www.pearsies.btinternet.co.uk

Bond Owners Club
www.bondownersclub.co.uk

Bond Bug
www.bondbug.com

Bristol Microcar Club
www.bristolmicrocarclub.com

Crosley
www.ggw.org/~cac/

Fiat 500
www.fiat500club.org.uk

Goggomobil
www.goggomobil.com

Heinkel/Trojan
www.heinkel-trojan-club.co.uk

Isetta Owners Club of Great Britain
www.isetta-owners-club-gb.com

Messerschmitt Enthusiasts Club
http://ourworld.compuserve.com/homep
ages/YatesAPJ/MEC_Home_Page.html

Messerschmitt Owners Club
www.messerschmitt.co.uk

Micromaniacs
www.micromaniacsclub.co.uk

Register of Unusual Microcars (RUM)
www.rumcars.org

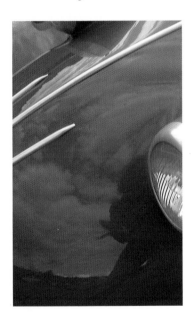

Reliant
www.reliantownersclub.co.uk

Scottish Microcar Club
www.scottishmicrocarclub.com

Sinclair C5
www.sinclair-research.co.uk/c5

Smart Club
www.thesmartclub.co.uk

Vespa 400
www.filnet.fr/perso/capaction/vespa.htm

Welsh Microcars
www.clwb-y-meicrocar.com

Argentina
Scooter & Microcar Club of Argentina
www.casym.com.ar

Japan
Isetta Owners Club of Japan
www.kiwat.com/isetta

Sweden
Microcar Club of Sweden
www.autosite.se/mcbil

USA/Canada
The Microcar and Minicar Club
www.microcar.org

Fiat 500 Owners Club of Canada
http://clubs.hemmings.com/frameset.cf
m?club=fiat500canada

selected museums, collections and events

Automuseum Störy (Germany)
www.automuseum-stoery.de

Auto Tron (The Netherlands)
www.autotron.nl

The Bruce Weiner Microcar Museum (US)
www.microcarmuseum.com

Classic Cars Live! (UK)
www.classiccarslive.com

Classic Motor Show (UK)
www.classiccarshow.co.uk

The Heritage Motor Centre (UK)
www.heritage.org.uk

The Lane Microcar Museum (US)
www.lanemotormuseum.org

The Museum of Automobile History (US)
www.themuseumofautomobilehistory.com

The National Motor Museum (UK)
www.beaulieu.co.uk/motormuseum

picture credits

A Harper
148-149

Automuseum Störy
70

Bob Bareham
55

Bob Nelson
115

Daihatsu Vehicle Distributors Ltd
backcover

David Appleton
58 (top left)

David Cowlard
frontcover (left and middle), 4, 42, 43
(bottom left and right), 59, 62-69, 72-81,
84-85, 88-89, 128, 135 (left)

Jacques Vuillaumier—CapAction
82-83

Mike Shepherd
47, 107 (bottom), 109 (bottom left),
125 (left), 137, 143-144, 154-157

Ray Glendinning
56-57

Register of Unusual Microcars
6, 7, 13-15, 17-18, 21, 40-41, 43
(top right), 44-46, 49, 94, 96-98,
103-105, 107 (top), 108, 109
(top and bottom right), 110, 112-114,
116-120, 123-124, 125 (right),
126-127, 129-134, 135 (right), 136,
138, 140-142, 145-147, 172-173

Richard Jones
87 (top left and right)

Steve Denning
60-61

Walter Zeichner
91

thanks

particular thanks go to:

Jean Hammond for her guidance, knowledge and advice.
Tony Marshall and Walter Zeichner for their time and
extensive knowledge.

David Cowlard for his time and skill in photographing
the owners and their cars.

thanks to:

Isabel Allen
Sonja Dahl
Claire Fox
Mark F Herbert
Sarah Jones
Lawrence and Jenny House
Jim Jamieson and the Micromaniacs
Richard Jones and the Isetta Club of Great Britain
Bob Nelson
John Meadows
Brian Richards
Mike Shepherd
Martha Rose Williams
All at Future Cities Project

Ken and Rhona Bell, Derek and Hazel Cole and Smart for
allowing their cars to feature on the cover.

All the owners and enthusiasts who have told their stories, provided
information, lent images and have allowed photographs to be taken
of themselves and their cars. Throughout the making of this book,
the owners have demonstrated, intentionally or not, that the microcar
community is a generous spirited one, populated with individuals only
too willing to offer help and guidance in order to lengthen the lives of
these cars and raise awareness of their significance.

At Draught Associates, Paul Stafford for his patience and dedication.

At Black Dog Publishing, Duncan McCorquodale for believing in the
book from the outset and for tireless support, and Tahani Nadim
for commitment above and beyond the ordinary.

colophon

Black Dog Publishing Limited

Architecture Art Design Fashion History
Photography Theory and Things

© 2004 Black Dog Publishing Limited

The authors and photographers have asserted their moral
right to the work comprising The Macro World of Microcars.

All rights reserved

Written by Kate Trant and Austin Williams
Designed by www.draught.co.uk
Printed in the European Union

Black Dog Publishing Limited
Unit 4.04 Tea Building
56 Shoreditch High Street
London E1 6JJ

T +44 (0)20 7613 1922
F +44 (0)20 7613 1944
E info@bdp.demon.co.uk
www.bdpworld.com

All opinions expressed within this publication are those
of the author and not necessarily of the publisher.

British Library Cataloguing-in-Publication Data.
A catalogue record for this book is available from the British Library.

ISBN 1 904772 04 8